AS A RESULT

A MEMOIR

D1600086

SARAH
BLIZZARD

Big Chief Books
Morgantown, West Virginia

As a Result © 2019 Big Chief Books, LLC

www.sarahblizzard.com

ISBN: 978-1-7327416-0-7

Production by:

Populore ®

Populore Publishing Company, Morgantown, West Virginia

Cover design: Jenna Britton

DEDICATION

— *To the memory of all those we have lost.*

— *To those who long for restoration. May you
find your way to wholeness and freedom.*

To Carol,
I'm so grateful
our writing paths have
crossed, and for your
support of my work.
May the "results" of our
words bring good rewards.
Blessings,
Sarah

Prologue

January 11, 1986.

THE PARTY'S FOR COUPLES. I show up alone.

"Where's Grant?" the hostess asks when she opens the door.

"I have no idea. He never came home from work."

The Japanese dinner party, which Beverly and her husband host in our neighborhood, is scheduled for six o'clock. I've lined up a sitter for our three-year-old. It's dark when the sitter shows up—right on time—but Grant still fails to surface. I pull on my snow boots, grab my coat and scarf, and march with purpose down the sidewalk.

I half-expect one of the oncoming cars to be his. But I arrive at the dinner party ten minutes later, a single. Beverly's husband takes my coat. I'm distracted by Beverly's ensemble: a full length, crimson-flowered, wrap-around kimono. A knitting needle pokes out of her bun.

"So, you're stag tonight?" she asks, tilting her dimpled smile at me. I nod and feel a cigarette craving come over me. "Oh, that's just Grant. Probably lost track of time. Caught up in some televised basketball on TV at Babe's Place. He'll come around."

"Maybe. But his office closed at three."

GRANT AND I HAD BECOME DRINKING PARTNERS just like my parents. The difference was that we were bar-hoppers, and our drinking behavior escalated—his faster than mine. Six years older than me, he'd had a head start. As the hangovers I suffered became worse, I slowed down. Grant could drink me under the table. I'd gotten used to not knowing where he was.

In the midst of our stupors, we had blowups that lasted for days. Six months earlier, I'd threatened to leave him. But instead of actually packing a bag, I called his mom. I needed to tell Margie where I was going and that I was taking her granddaughter. Grant's mom had been our primary babysitter. It was close to midnight, but I called her anyway.

"It's me," I said through my tears. "Grant just came home. No explanation. I've had it. I'm leaving and taking the baby to my parents' house." Mom and Dad lived about a three-hour drive away.

"I'm coming right over," she said. She arrived minutes later and sat next to me on the sofa. She spoke softly, made no judgments.

"Leaving is the easy thing to do. Staying and working things out is harder. If you leave, if this leads to divorce, it will be like a death."

I stayed.

Now, at the dinner party, I realize I've grown quite fond of Grant's friends, all of whom grew up together and are older than me. But Grant's the one who has the history with these people. I light up a smoke and inhale deeply. Maybe I shouldn't have come.

As the other guests arrive, I make my way to the kitchen where Beverly's husband pours me a stiff drink. The dinner guests' welcoming chatter increases as I attempt to squelch my feeling of abandonment. I take a gulp of the vodka and OJ, and look for an ashtray.

On another snowy January evening eight years earlier, January 1978, Grant and I had said, "I do." His friends said the words a love-struck, nineteen-year-old, codependent girl-child wants to hear: "You're so good for Grant."

Grant exudes confidence. He's the number-one salesman at his company. He advances to small business ownership. Our daughter is healthy, smart, and charming, and an answer to prayer after the devastating loss of our first baby. When Amy died, Grant and I had leaned on each other. Neither of us blamed the other. Still, I was guilt-ridden. There were times I'd cared more about the wallpaper that went on her nursery walls than what was best for her. I had no tools to deal with grief. I stuffed it deep and put a tight lid on it.

I HELP BEVERLY SET THE TABLE. As we finish the egg rolls, we hear the front door open. Grant enters but is far too drunk to socialize. When Beverly tries to talk to him, he waves her away. This isn't the time for me to demand an explanation. Besides, I'm tired of sounding like a shrew. A few minutes later, Grant and his friend Buddy disappear out into the cold.

I grab my coat. Beverly says, "I'll call you tomorrow."

When I arrive home, Grant and Buddy are at the front door. I pay the sitter. Buddy and I help Grant upstairs. I sleep downstairs on the couch.

The next morning, Beverly calls. She and Patty, another friend of Grant's, want to come over.

"You need help, man!" Beverly says the minute she sees him. Grant has made his way downstairs; he sits up straight in the chair and lets out a long sigh. "We're worried about you. You're completely out of control."

"What are you going to do?" the women ask me as Grant heads upstairs, and I lead them to the front door. I just shake my head. I close the door and hear Grant's scratchy voice call for me.

"Hmmm?" I say from the bedroom door.

"That guy Mike, what's his number?" he asks. Mike and his wife, Jill, had graduated from a reputable rehab. Jill's sister was one of our drinking buddies. I toss him the phone book and suggest he look it up. Grant raises up on an elbow. The phone's next to the bed. I make myself scarce gathering laundry. I sense our problems are bigger than both of us, but when I hear him actually dial the number, I freeze.

Mike and Jill pull up fifteen minutes later. It's as if they'd been expecting Grant's call. They stand at the front door eager to help. I invite them in, and they sit side by side on our sofa. Our daughter plays in the far corner of the dining room, distracted by her plastic dollhouse with its imaginary family, which I hope isn't as dysfunctional as the one in which she's being raised.

"If you really want to stop drinking," Jill says, "there's help available."

"To be honest," Mike continues, "we've already made some arrangements at a rehab near Reading, an hour's flight from Pittsburgh. Same place we attended. There's a room for you." Grant hangs his head. With a barely perceptible nod, he gives their plan his consent.

"In the meantime," Jill says, looking directly at me, "you might want to consider attending Al-Anon." I'd heard of AA and Al-Anon but had preconceived notions about them as places for very unhappy people. But I soon discover Al-Anon meetings are for those who love an alcoholic. I qualify in spades.

WHEN I WALK INTO THE FELLOWSHIP HALL of the old church on Wheeling Island the next day, everyone's a stranger to me except Melissa, the woman sitting at the end of the table. We'd been in the same training class for Crisis Hotline the year before. I don't speak directly to her, but I share that this is my first meeting.

"I think I need this," I say through tears. "My husband is at rehab right now. That's where he needs to be. But I know I need support. Things have been terrible between us for a long while, and we have a young daughter." Someone hands me the tissues.

Everyone there can relate to what it feels like to attend a meeting for the first time. I feel their compassion. The theme of the evening is "Let Go and Let God." I like what Melissa has to say. Afterward, people give me phone numbers that I can call for support, day or night, especially while my husband is away. I think about speaking directly to Melissa.

She's blind but might recognize my voice. I introduce myself.

"I remember you from Crisis Hotline," I say. "Could I have your phone number and call you sometime?" She's receptive, and I call her soon afterward. I continue going to meetings where members share their strengths, explain catchy slogans like "Live and Let Live" and "One Day at a Time." I buy a meditation book called *One Day at a Time in Al-Anon,* and when they all stand to hold hands and pray the Our Father, I join them. When they say, "Let us love you until you can learn to love yourself," I wonder, *How do they know I don't love myself?*

LATER THAT WEEK, Grant's recovery counselor calls. "He says he wants to come home."

Wait. It's only been a week. The counselor continues, "This is contrary to the plans we feel are best for him, but he's free to go. We want to know how you feel about it."

I know exactly how I feel, which surprises me. Without hesitation, I express my honest assessment of how our marriage is in danger of dissolving under the weight of our actions and of how we both deserve a chance, and that chance depends on us making a concerted effort. I mention that I've begun to attend Al-Anon meetings. The counselor thanks me and hangs up.

Grant calls later that evening. He's angry. He wants to bargain. "I can come home and go to meetings. I can take care of my own problems." I repeat what I told his counselor. Then I surprise myself when I say, "Look, I've made a decision, and I'm not turning back. I'm going to Al-Anon like it's my job. No matter what you decide, I can not—will not—return to how we were living. If you insist on coming home before the twenty-eight days are up, all your things will be out on the front porch. And the locks will be changed. I can't live under the same roof with you, not like it's been." He hangs up.

I

Background Check

MOM ALWAYS RESPONDED CURTLY to probing questions about her father and his death at a young age. "He owed a gambling debt. He was killed. It was a case of mistaken identity." Only years after Mom died did my sister Hannah go to the Huntington, West Virginia, main library and find a news report on microfilm about our grandfather. At age twenty-three, our grandfather lost his young life after a terrible fight. He had gone into a run-down neighborhood to pawn a pearl-handled pistol for moonshine whiskey. The fight ensued and someone, or maybe the sidewalk, cracked his head open. He died later at the hospital. There are plenty of loose ends to this dramatic ending, not the least of which was what became of the man who fought with our grandfather. He went to jail, and my sister never did get back to learn the rest of the story. We figured Mom's family, all teetotaling Methodists, were mortified by the entire episode. Maybe Mom knew only what she'd been told. In any case, when asked about her childhood, Mom would get a faraway look in her eyes and say, "My life began when I met your father."

MOM'S MOTHER WAS WIDOWED in her mid-twenties and left to raise three small children. Mom, who was three, was the youngest. Her maternal grandparents, with whom she grew up, the Wilsons, had thirteen children and lived on a farm outside of Huntington. There were occasional whispers about Mom's brother and sister, about abuse

Mom's sister suffered, police reports of a missing uncle, authorities at the door flashing IDs, and Mom's cry that she had no "earthly idea" where her brother might be.

Our most famous relative on Mom's side was a second cousin, with whom Mom shares a maternal grandfather. Mary Eloise Vinson married Lucien Philip Smith, the son of a wealthy coal family from Morgantown. The couple was returning home from an extended European honeymoon in April 1912 on the doomed *Titanic*, and Lucien was among the hundreds of passengers and crew members drowned. His pregnant young widow, Mary Eloise, became a reluctant celebrity in Huntington, especially when she had to testify concerning the ship's last hours. Mom told us about Mary Eloise and taught us the "The *Titanic*," which we sang with gusto on long car trips. It was safe to sing of this ancestor.

> *It was sad, when the great ship went down*
> *to the bottom of the sea;*
> *Husbands lost their wives;*
> *Little children lost their lives.*

DAD'S BACKGROUND IS EASIER TO ASCERTAIN. His surname, Blizzard, is ancient and means "wielders of the broadsword." I picture ghostly ancestors with weapons and personalities as fierce as the snowstorms we associate with our name; phantom storms in the flesh. We trace our lineage back to Sir William Blizzard, 1743–1835, famed for his role in a rebellion against the Crown.

Ancestral Blizzards were heroic leaders: Thomas fought with the cavalry in Jamestown and Yorktown; John moved to America and acquired land in Pendleton County, West Virginia. Down the line came Dad's infamous cousin Bill Blizzard, a pioneer in the organization of union workers and the hero of the Battle of Blair Mountain, where he commanded a coal miners' army.

Dad's grandmother was pregnant with twins when her husband lost a dreadful battle with logs on Paint Creek. Dad's father was five at the time. He had one sibling, an older sister.

Dad's mom had hands the size of a man's and skills she'd gleaned in her youth at the beginning of the twentieth century. She learned sewing crafts and was well-trained on canning, food preservation, and other homemaking projects at her 4-H camp at Jackson's Mill.

By the time Dad came of age, my grandfather had worked his way to power-crew leader at the Appalachia Power Company and saw a place for his sure-footed, six-foot-two, two-hundred-pound son. It must've been the summer of 1938 when Dad joined the company of men who traveled by way of deeply rutted roads and tight hogback turns to work sites in the mountains of West Virginia. The crew of older men, including many uncles and cousins, formed a fraternity of sorts. The crew leaders strapped Dad with the wire he had to string across a ravine or from one mountainside to the next—through perilous paths and steep hillsides where black bears hibernate a few extra weeks. It was his job to string cable wires the size of thick ropes, lift them like weights from mountainside to crest, valley to hill, all the while listening to his fellow crewmen's deep voices echoing in the canyons.

Before he left for Marshall College, graduated, married my mom, and joined the US Navy, Dad understood survival skills, the power of electricity, positive from negative, and the life secrets that young men learn from being in an exclusive men's club. He absorbed brutal ideas about life and death. An outdoorsman and a hunter, he'd no problem shooting a desperately wounded animal and putting it out of its misery. The crew likely offered him swigs of whiskey, cultivated Scotch-Irish traditions, and inspired his "poor dog songs" of Rover and Jack, which he sang at the breakfast table but we kids never quite understood.

Dad and Mom both studied at Marshall College, Dad in engineering and Mom in home economics. Despite their vastly different fields of study, they found themselves in one of the same classes. Mom, hurrying to her desk, didn't notice the guy behind her. Once she was seated, she realized that her skirt was folded up under her. She needed to readjust and smooth out the pleats or they wouldn't lie right. So, she lifted up her hips from her chair and began to make a smoothing motion with her hands. Dad's big Oxford lace-up shoes happened to be resting on the bottom rung of her chair. Once Mom lifted herself, his long legs thrust her chair forward and she plopped back down with a *thump!*

Turning to give the offender a mean look, Mom laid eyes on Dad, a curly-headed, blue-eyed engineering student. He sat forward in his seat and smiled. His lower lip was naturally thick and the corners of his mouth rose up slightly in an all-knowing way. They were an item from that moment on.

I WONDER AT TIMES if our parents had ever really planned to have six kids. When Dad was in the navy, he and Mom lived in navy housing at Penney Farms near St. Augustine, Florida. When Dad went to sea, the other women in base housing took Mom under their wing and taught her to play bridge. The young couple had three children: Rosemary, Molly, and Ed, their prized third child who satisfied his proud father's urge for a son he could teach to fish and hunt and become a man.

When Dad completed his service, he moved the family to Dunbar, West Virginia, across the street from his parents. One summer day years before I was born, when Ed was seven and running across the street to Granny's, he was hit by a car. He lay in a coma for days on end. Adults spoke in hushed tones, and Molly and Rosemary got no updates on their little brother's condition. When Ed finally awakened, he had a steel pin implanted in his leg bone and enough broken bones to warrant a full body cast with just openings for bathroom needs. Mom kept the news clipping that featured a photo of her boy propped up on his elbows in bed and reading, his cute butt peeking out behind that massive cast. He was homeschooled for a year.

With three children, the youngest of whom had undergone significant trauma, it might appear the family was complete. But when Ed was eight, Hannah appeared, the first of another trio that would be born to the family within a thirty-month period. Less than two years later, John arrived a month early and almost died due to Mom's placenta previa. With each new birth, Mom was drawn away from Dad, a husband sorely lacking in empathy or compassion to care for a fragile and vulnerable child. Within months she was pregnant, again, with me.

During this pregnancy, Dad accepted a new job with the power company and moved the family from Dunbar. His eleven-year-old son helped him convert the garage of the new brick bungalow in Lebanon, Virginia, into a family room. Was that when Dad bought Ed that special gift, that genuine rawhide whip that he learned to snap out toward Rosemary and Molly whenever he wanted to hear them scream?

Sing Me to Sleep

ROSEMARY'S SIXTEEN, Molly, fourteen; Ed, eleven; Hannah, three, and John is fourteen months when I'm born in 1959. Mom's doctor tells her not to come back if she gets pregnant again. He doesn't think she can take it, or maybe he can't. She admits that without the older three, she couldn't possibly manage. When Rosemary, Molly, and Ed get off the school bus at 3:00, they take one look at Mom and say, "For heaven's sake, Mom. Go lie down." And she does, for a while, before starting supper.

Dad has a vasectomy, and Mom's ecstatic about never again getting pregnant. In photos from that time—at my baptism, and during our trips to the beach—she exhibits a new mirth. Whenever anyone asks if she's pregnant again, she replies, "Sweetie, if I'm pregnant, it would be an act of God."

Our family's life in the Virginia Highlands is just beginning, and I seem to be born aware of everything going on around me. Even as I play with the string of colored beads attached to a bar on the front tray of my blue-green stroller, I pick up on family dynamics. By the time I can walk and talk, John is my best buddy. We seek one another out inside and outside of our cozy brick bungalow.

When she's done with diapers, Mom relaxes. She's five foot two and trim—a happy homemaker in her skirt and simple blouse, her apron tied around her waist like a uniform. She's generally level-headed, well-read, and highly respected by her three oldest. She's always in a good mood. She's a great cook and prepares well-balanced meals from scratch following recipes in her grease-stained *Fannie Farmer Cookbook*. Occasionally she takes a cigarette break with one of her unfiltered Camels. I watch as she takes a deep drag, then removes a piece of tobacco no bigger than a piece of confetti from the tip of her tongue with her pinkie. But her break won't last long. She snuffs the fiery end into an overflowing ashtray and is back on her feet until after supper. She has very little social life. On rare occasions, she's invited somewhere to play bridge.

A strapping man, Dad towers over Mom. The steel-lunchbox-carrying dad of the 1950s, he can be gruff and angry when we act up, or he can be a teddy bear when I climb into his lap as he sits on the couch. He's a supervisor at the power plant, a troubleshooter and a man's man. He gets along well supervising his comrades. He wears pocketed shirts to hold his filtered Raleigh cigarettes. The stainless-steel lighter is dwarfed by his large hand: he opens, lights up, and closes the little contraption with three exact flicks of his right thumb. Each evening, he and Mom sit in the living room and she listens to the stories of his day. He unwinds with one glass of whiskey after another. Most nights, Mom keeps up.

WE VISIT GRANNY in Green Bank in the remote, mountainous region of Pocahontas County, West Virginia. Granny's hands are seldom idle: she quilts, crochets, and cooks better than anyone, which Mom attests to whenever comparing her skills with her mother-in-law's.

Just across the way from Granny's farm on North Fork Road is a 300-foot telescope that's part of the National Radio Astronomy Observatory. Granny puts us on a tour bus so we can see it up close. "They can track unusual sounds coming from outer space," says the tour guide. "Wow," John says. "Outer space!" Our only reference is a black and white

TV show, "Lost in Space," about a robot and astronauts who land on another planet. The telescope that replaces the 300-foot one is 485-feet tall and is the world's largest fully steerable radio telescope.

The historic Cass Scenic Railroad is nearby, too. One day we take the long, noisy ride to the top of a mountain on the old steam engine. I cover my ears to the shrillest whistle I've ever heard and the sound of the steel wheels turning along the centuries-old tracks.

Granny takes us to a chicken farm. We come back with two live ones still clucking. Granny twists their scrawny necks (pop!) and plunges them feathers and all into a pot of scalding water. After she plucks them naked, her hands are covered with light gray feathers.

With those same hands, she kneads dough, shapes it into rolls, and delivers them hot from the oven, next to the best fried chicken I'd ever tasted. I try not to think of the violence those birds underwent in order for us to eat. By evening, her wood stove is on its last log. In its embers are remnants of the sausage she canned, which she served with buckwheat cakes that morning.

The last time we stay with Granny on the farm, Grandpa has passed away, never again to be seen sitting in his rocker next to a roaring fire, smoking his pipe and warming his toes.

HANNAH AND I SHARE A LARGE BEDROOM with Rosemary and Molly, separated by a wall-sized accordion-pleated partition that folds back. At bedtime, after Hannah quits talking and falls asleep, I curl up under the quilt in my single bed. I hear a noise and I pull the covers up over my nose, leaving just my eyes to peek out. Halloween has passed, but all the scary images of witches and skeletons linger in my mind. I hear someone: either Rosemary or Molly returning from a date. I relax now, lie quietly and listen for clues as to which of my sisters is back.

I watch the ceiling above the partition for any sign of illumination. Outside my window, the wind sweeps up a pile of leaves. A street lamp casts a dim glow inside our bedroom. Long shadows begin a light show; my eyes widen to the spooky dance on the wall's vertical screen. Please hurry, sister! *If that really is my sister.* She should be in her room by now. What's taking her so long? I'm rigid in my bed, waiting for signs of life on the other side of the room. If it's Molly, she's probably looking in the mirror, pretending she's kissing her boyfriend. I hear the shuffling of shoes. Finally! Though I'm still not sure which sister it is. I try to guess by the shadows I spy on the ceiling: her elbows up; hands removing bobby pins one by one. Then arms lifted again, hands to hair. Is that the brush I detect, the new one Mom bought from the Fuller Brush man? Molly had teased her bobbed hair that evening. Before her date showed up, it stuck straight out in every direction. Before she calmed it down, Ed said it was bound to pick up a signal from outer space.

From my side of the partition I hear a throat being cleared. It's Molly. I call out for her. She sits by my pillow. "Sing the Charlie song," I say, though I don't really understand the words. She sings me to sleep with the haunting Kingston Trio ballad, the one where a man's fate changes at some point because he keeps getting on some train and he never, ever gets off. Another favorite, "Five Hundred Miles," might be even more depressing: "Not a shirt on my back, not a penny to my name, Lord, I can't go back home this ole way. Lord, I'm one, Lord, I'm two, Lord, I'm three, Lord, I'm four, Lord, I'm five hundred miles away from home." The songs make me feel homesick, though I've not left my bed. But Molly's soothing voice lulls me into a sound sleep.

My parents glow with favor for Rosemary. Of Molly, their second born, Mom repeatedly says, "If she'd been born first, I never would've had another one." In front of Molly, Mom lists all the ways Molly drives her crazy. "She always tries to get out of doing any work! There's just no pleasing her!" Even as a child, I'm embarrassed to hear Mom speak this way. She and Dad draw attention to Molly's weight and encourage her to lose her extra pounds.

Molly, who is like a second mother to me, refuses to live in Rosemary's shadow. She's very popular at school, an excellent student, and outspoken.

In 1962, when I'm three, Rosemary, nineteen, is married. She looks like a princess in her long, white satin wedding gown. Sophisticated and charming, Rosemary has striking, emerald eyes, and a golden-tan complexion. As Dogwood Festival Queen, a pretty big deal in our rural community, she was escorted by Bob Denver, who played Gilligan on *Gilligan's Island*. Rosemary's future husband, Geoffrey, is the son of a local doctor we call "Dr. Geoffrey." Tall and slim in his fitted suit, my new brother-in-law looks debonair in his wedding attire.

Rosemary's departure from home coincides with my first viewing of *The Wizard of Oz*. The wedding and the film create a jumble in my mind that shapes a bizarre dream: Mom takes Hannah, John, and me to a doctor's office. We're all in the waiting room, and there's a two-way mirror/window on the wall. We can see in to the next room, but the people in that room cannot see us. All of a sudden, I see my sister flying around the room on a broomstick, like she's training to be a witch. It's not a scary dream, just a dream about Rosemary taking broom-flying lessons and leaving us.

When they return from their honeymoon in New England, they bring an old mantel clock that doesn't work. "Let me have a stab at it," Dad says. That exchange marks the beginning of what will become Dad's lifelong obsession with antique clocks. He takes the thing apart and figures out the complicated inner workings. He schedules his two-week summer vacation in Cape Cod where he establishes a repertoire with the help of antique shop proprietors. In coming years, he will acquire empty wooden clock cases and bring home an assemblage of gears, bellows, chains, and weights. He'll collect and repair, as needed, all manner of timepieces, including pocket watches and an assortment of shapely, sand-filled hourglasses. Some weight-driven clocks in ornate wooden cases hang on our walls. Others we call mantel clocks fill counter spaces, and still others, stately cottage and grandfather clocks, stand in the corners of our living room like stationary pets.

Rosemary's departure signifies a turning point in Mom and Dad's child-rearing. They see the light at the end of a very long tunnel. They become adult friends with Rosemary and Geoffrey. Geoffrey graduates from law school, and Rosemary becomes a homemaker.

MY FAMILY PRAISES MY INQUISITIVENESS and personality. Dad tells me on occasion, "You're going to be Miss America." They think I'm some kind of genius when they find me, age four, sitting up in my bed reading Molly's trigonometry book. I'm drawn to the geometric drawings. Whether or not I'm a genius, I feel important and valued.

Molly falls in love with Robby, and I beg her and Robby to take me places in his Volkswagen and include me on their dates to the drive-in theater. Molly usually says, "Not this time." But Robby smiles and tells her, "She's okay. Let her come with us." I develop a strong bond with him. I can be myself with him. From my toilet seat, I yell, "Robby, come wipe me!" I never live down that line. In 1963, when I'm four, Molly and Robby marry.

With Rosemary and Molly married, life in our home settles into a busy routine. Some days bring more trouble for John than usual. Too often, he sets himself up for a spanking. Hannah and I get in our share of trouble. But, even when all three of us act up, and Dad walks down the road to cut a switch from a tree, we know that John will get the worst of it.

Ed is my hero. He plays football, has his driver's license, sneaks cigarettes, and attends formal dances with the beautiful Lee West. At the same time, good times with Ed hold a mix of torture and tension, like the Saturday afternoon that he walks Hannah, John, and me the half mile to Lebanon's local movie theater for the matinee *The Pit and the Pendulum*. We've already seen *Mary Poppins*. We sit in a middle row. The music is eerie as the scene unfolds. Vincent Price straps his powerless victim to a table and a gigantic curved blade descends from the ceiling, swinging like the pendulums on Dad's clocks. The blade falls closer and closer to the man's abdomen and cuts through the man's skin. I hold a death grip on my armrest.

Though the movie is in black and white, I picture everything as if it's in vivid color. I walk home as fast as my legs will carry me, tortured by vivid, bloody images. Only the comfort of home can replace my terrifying thoughts. In our kitchen, Mom is slathering ketchup on baloney sandwiches. All I see is blood. I run crying from the table.

Hannah, three years older than me, is really bright. On an IQ test, she scores the highest marks in Russell County.

John, the fifth born, shares a room and bunk beds with Ed. John is my closest sibling and best friend. From early on, each of the six of us is defined by a word or two. Rosemary and sometimes Hannah are high achievers. Hannah and Ed are mediators. John and sometimes Molly are scapegoats. Rosemary and I are mascots; and, always, I am the tattletale.

I value my siblings and can't imagine my life without any one of them, but I would rat them out in a second. I see Ed light up a smoke. My parents forbid this. I can't wait to announce what I've seen. Already, I can read Dad, and my fickle allegiance to any one of my siblings changes depending on the circumstances. I'm smart enough to redirect Dad's attention towards them so I remain his little buddy. It's all about survival and all around me are victims whose imminent peril I can identify with.

Like the Easter egg incident. John may be fourteen months older, but we're equals, and mostly, John lets me lead. But on this Easter when we're both still little, he gets us in big trouble. He suggests we load up every one of the pastel, hard-boiled Easter eggs from the platter on which they rest on the kitchen table. Mom is washing dishes, her back turned. We fill our jacket pockets and go outside to crack off their shells.

One by one, we throw the eggs as high as we can at our brick house, just to see if they'll stick. I then return to the house and tell Mom: "Did you know John and I have been crackin' those colored Easter eggs, the ones missin' from the center of the kitchen table? We're throwin' them up against the house, and they're stickin' to the brick!"

Mom shoots me an angry look. Then she calls for Ed to haul a ladder to the side of the house where he spends an hour scrubbing away all those pieces of hard-boiled egg.

"Go straight to your rooms, right this minute! There'll be no Easter dinner for either of you," Mom scolds, her arms outstretched. We're banished to our rooms for the day. The scent of ham, potato casserole and rolls wafts down the hallway. I believe I can hear Hannah enjoying her slice of homemade cake.

I have to take charge. When John pees outside, I tell Mom: "Mom, John peed outside again." John gets spanked. But, no matter what, he's my best friend. My inner child and his merge. Our hearts and minds forge a twin-like pattern. We love and trust one another.

. . . I'm two years old. I toddle up to my mom's elbow. She sits at the card table catty-corner from Dad. They're playing their nightly card game. I stretch up on tiptoe. I see their drinks and reach for Mom's. She holds the glass for me while I take a big gulp. When she tries to pull it away, I resist, tightly clutching the glass and begging for one more sip. She indulges me. She laughs when her bourbon doesn't seem to faze me. When I shiver, she takes the glass away. I sleep soundly those nights . . .

Burned Out

"**WAKE UP! WAFFLES ARE READY!**" John appears next to my bed; his stuffed monkey is clutched in the crook of his elbow like a rag doll. I've been waiting for him to wake me ever since the sun's rays came peeping through my bedroom window.

"Is today Sunday?" I ask, sitting up. John holds the monkey to my face; makes it nod. I yawn as I push his friend away and hop out. "After breakfast, we have mass." I scurry down the hallway after my brother, toward the sound and smell of sizzling bacon.

"By the time we get back," he says, pouring syrup all over his plate, "Dad'll be in the workshop." Dad never attends church with us. "Pray for me," he always says. On Sundays, he makes things and drinks bourbon.

Finishing the last bite, John takes a gulp of milk and wipes his creamy mustache away with his hand. "I'm gonna see if he'll let me use his measuring tape," John says. He just wants to see how much taller he is than me.

DAD'S SHOP isn't exactly a basement; it's more like an over-sized root cellar that he and Ed dug out when Mom was expecting me. Once we enter the windowless room, it takes a minute for my eyes to adjust. The floor is as tight as cement, packed-down from Dad's size 11 work shoes. The hard ground glistens in reddish-brown Virginia clay and stains the bottoms of our bare feet the color of the burnt sienna crayon in my Crayola box. At six three, Dad has to duck a bit as he moves about. We don't dare get a toe in his way when he crosses the room searching for something in a shadowy corner. He picks up what looks like a ruler from some shelf. He sits down on a low stool at his plywood table and goes to work sharpening a saw with the ruler-thingy. The shop air is cool. It smells of oil and metal. John searches for the measuring tape while I stand still watching Dad tighten a bare lightbulb that hangs straight down from a black wire attached to a hook in the dirt ceiling. My brother loses interest in the tape when he can't figure out which end to start with or how it even works, so we wander back outdoors and leave Dad to tinker all by himself.

It's an Indian summer's day, dry and sticky, with no rain in sight. I fill my shorts pockets with black walnuts in their shells, gathering them from underneath our gigantic tree. Then I find a white rock that can act as chalk and draw a hopscotch pattern on the driveway. I hop on one foot, drop a walnut shell into a square, and turn to pick it up, never once losing my balance. Out of the corner of my eye, I notice Dad leaving his shop. A page from my "*Fun with Dick and Jane*" reader comes to mind, the one with the dad mowing the lawn.

"*Away I go,*" *said Father.*

A few minutes later, Dad walks back into his cave with a drink. I plop down in the middle of the driveway, and black walnuts spill out of my shorts pockets. I need Dad's hammer to break open the shells, but I hesitate when I hear the screeching buzz of his electric saw blade and see sawdust flying out the door like a swarm of gold gnats.

"*Look, oh, look. See them go.*"

The next time I see Dad shuffling down the yard, he's freshened his drink again. Maybe he'll give me a sip. But he stops to make a funny face when he sees me staring. I giggle when he juts out his chin, using his tongue to pop out his false teeth. His bottom dentures hang at the end of his lips like they're gonna fall out. Then he sucks them back in, but not before I spy the shiny pink plastic underneath his fake teeth. John and I laugh as we pull at our own teeth, but they won't budge. As he ducks back into his shop, Dad whistles a tune, and we file in behind him like we're following the Pied Piper. When he sets down his drink after taking a big swig, the liquor is the same burnt sienna as the shop floor.

Our eyes light up when we realize Dad's latest project is a Santa Claus: a life-sized, mechanical, battery-operated, super-hero that will rock side-to-side and wave to our neighbors every Christmas season from his perch on the side of our house.

John and I stand on tiptoes, watching Dad concentrate. He applies a generous stream of wood glue across the middle of Santa's red suit, then affixes a trim piece of plywood, tightening a vise around the jolly old man. Every rotation by Dad's thick, strong hands is precise: turn, turn, turn, but not too tight.

Waiting to see the finished Santa is like waiting for Christmas Eve, so we head to the house and wash up for quick peanut butter sandwiches.

Back outdoors, a not so itsy-bitsy daddy longlegs crawls up the back of my brother's white undershirt. I reach up and wave the spider off. But when John feels my fingers brush his back, he turns around, following the daddy's path as it high-steps along the yard on its own stilts.

"Don't lose him, he's mine!" John yells, picking up the weightless creature and, mimicking it, high-steps out into the field, letting the bug crawl up his hand. He smiles as it tickles the hairs on his arm. When he finally flicks it off, John finds a long stick like the switch Dad sometimes uses on the back of our legs. Scratching it along the driveway, John pesters a wooly caterpillar, coaxing it out of a crack. But the creature doesn't like the switch either, so he curls up, refusing to play with us. We run back into Dad's cave to check on Santa's progress.

Santa stands propped up against the wall next to a fan slowly drying his glue. The piece of wood scrap has become the jolly man's belt:

Dad's already painted it black with a silver buckle. Loose arms and legs on hinges will be attached like real joints. Dad grabs a hammer off the shelf, and with a ping-ping-ping, taps the hinges into place.

BY LATE AFTERNOON, Dad has made countless trips indoors. When he returns the last time, the sun is low in the sky. His lower lip is swollen. He carries a can of Zippo lighter fluid, the one he usually keeps under the kitchen sink for filling his and Mom's cigarette lighters. He holds the can in one hand; in the other is a stick with a rag wrapped around it. He staggers to the base of the black walnut tree and lights the rag with his Zippo lighter. He reaches up with the torch, setting fire to a big worm nest on a branch.

A gust of wind blows up dirt in every direction. The unexpected air current clips off the dead branch, along with the cluster of gray cobwebs, the ones with sizzling worms. The leaves on the black walnut tree spring to life, clapping their hands like tambourines. The breeze coaxes the leaves to become partners in a fiery, autumn hoedown. I hold still, shielding my eyes with my bent arm from a sudden assault of smoke, but it finds its way up my nose. I pull my T-shirt up over my face and run towards the driveway.

Moments later, adults run toward us screaming, "The field's on fire!" I smell lighter fluid and spy flickering embers like daylight fireflies. Maybe Dad should've picked a calmer day.

John and I obey Mom's voice urging us toward the house. We run with our heads turned back toward the spectacle: pop-up blazes light new fires along the dry reeds in the open field where we play cowboys and Indians with our friends. The fires play leap frog above our favorite hill, the one we sled down in winter.

Mom unwinds the garden hose and pulls it taut to the backyard. Neighbors come running with pails. "Over here!" someone shouts. People form a line from a neighbor's water spigot. Ours is at full throttle.

Buckets-to-hands, hands-to-buckets; turn and pass them quickly to the next person, like a game of hot potato. The buckets are too small for such a big fire.

In the distance, a screeching siren sounds. In minutes, a gigantic red fire truck pulls into Lebanon Manor and barrels up our gravel road where our old dog had been lying. Fritzy moves in the nick of time!

"Run, Spot, run!"

John and I stay indoors at the picture window as the firemen smother the last of the flames and rewind their hoses. By nightfall, everyone returns home. Mom says it was a close call. Dad is awfully quiet. All that's left of the field is a wet, smoky expanse of charred sticks. But our yard, the house, and all of us remain unharmed. Santa is intact. We are young and innocent and unaware of what we and the black walnut tree have survived.

Cowboys and Indians

JOHN AND I ARE INNOCENT PRESCHOOLERS, and like most children of our era, we love to play cowboys and Indians with neighbors and friends. During one game, a heavyset thirteen-year-old boy runs up behind me and yells, "Lie down, you've been shot! I have to take the bullet out." When I drop to the ground, he pulls down my pants and fondles me. Other kids are running all around us. Most of them just run off. I assume he does this to them, too, and that it must be my turn. When he leaves, I pull up my pants and run to join the others.

One day when this happens again, another playmate stops running and says to me, "Sarah, don't ever let him do that to you again. It's wrong!" So, I do what I always do. I tattle. I run to the boy's house. His little brother is my playmate, and I tell my playmate to go tell their mother exactly what his brother has done. I sit on the ottoman in their family room listening. I can hear her in the kitchen yelling at her older son. Her anger empowers me. I know the boy will never touch me again. What I don't know is that John, too, is one of this boy's victims. But John never tattles. He never feels the power that I feel to make it stop. And it doesn't stop.

LEBANON, VIRGINIA, in 1964, with its farmland and high plains right outside our window, gives us a sense of space, perspective, and a panoramic view of the Appalachian Mountains and foothills. John, Hannah, and I play on the driveway or at the neighbor's. We ride bikes up our gravel road. When I can't find John, I spend the day at my friend Meredith's house or play outside with our next-door neighbor, Luke. When it rains, we jump around in his family room, Luke in his Mighty Mouse cape, leaping from couch to ottoman and back again.

One day, Luke and I take a walk out past the big burned-down field. He follows close behind me on a well-beaten trail. When we come upon a long, springy limb blocking our path, I push the limb full of thorny sticks forward and move through. When it springs back, it catches him on his eyeball. He grabs at his eye and screams. We run back to his house and show his mom the dark red streak on Luke's eye. I'd never seen an eye bleed before. I feel terrible, but neither Luke nor his mom blame me.

During those Virginia summers we play kick-the-can in the middle of the road, moving aside only for slow-moving vehicles. Some days, Mom rounds us up and we pile into the family car, the windows rolled down, for a trip to nearby Hungry Mother State Park. We take a picnic and sometimes stay for a dip in the lake.

When Hannah's eight, she scares everybody when she comes walking home on a sunny afternoon in the midst of a group of her playmates. Her platinum blonde hair is coated with blood. Dark red streaks cascade down from the part on the top of her head, already matting the sides. A boy Hannah's been playing with boldly carries the hammer that he's just used to hit my sister over the head. Since Hannah walks under her own power, we figure she's okay. And she is, though mightily offended, as anyone would be who'd been hit hard for no reason. Mom rushes to the scene. Hannah becomes more selective of her friends. But the dangers lurking around our little Lebanon Manor are not to be ignored.

I begin having vivid encounters with an imaginary friend named Big Chief. When I'm supposed to be napping, I play with the six-foot-tall

Indian warrior, who stands in the corner of my bedroom with his arms folded with authority across his chest. He has a most commanding, full-feathered headdress. Big Chief is my superhero, my guardian angel. Mom indulges me. She sets a place for Big Chief at the supper table.

"**WASH UP!**" Mom calls one evening around supper time. She holds open the screen door as we rush inside. It might be hot dogs, with homemade chili sauce and fresh coleslaw Mom has grated herself and mixed with the perfect blend of mayonnaise and onion, a little mustard, evaporated milk, salt, pepper, and sugar. I know because I often climb up on a stool and move in right next to her elbow to study her whenever she lets me watch her cook.

But this supper is even better than hot dogs. Granny's homemade apple butter, given to us the last time we were in Pocahontas County visiting Dad's mom, sits open on the table. Aromas of Mom's tender pot roast, biscuits, potatoes, and carrots greet us in our homey, knotty-pine kitchen. Four of us kids usually sit on the ladder-back chairs at the sturdy, round oak table—unless John is doing penance for taking a pee outside, in which case only three of us fill our plates. Mom and Dad have begun to skip our early supper. Their highballs and card games come first.

Nearing sunset, right before bedtime, Ed and the Lerner brothers gather in their blue jeans, tucked-in T-shirts, hands in their pockets; an audience of handsome teenage boys for my wobbly attempts at riding a two-wheeler. Ed follows me on the gravel road, his hand attached to my bike seat until I steady myself. I bite my lower lip in concentration. The boys laugh at my Norman-Rockwell-painting expression and freckled face. I'm determined to make that hand-me-down bike balance itself with me on it. I weave down the entire length of our road, stop, turn, and return unassisted. Ed crows, "Look at you go!" His voice is ringing in my ear when I'm in the bath and Mom discovers purplish polka-dot bruises caused by bouncing incessantly on that worn-out bicycle seat over that gravel road.

On most Friday mornings, Mom takes John and me with her on the weekly shopping trip to Abingdon, Virginia. One day, Mom lets us loose in the Piggly Wiggly grocery store. She's concentrating on fresh fruit and vegetables in the produce section. Up one aisle and down the other, John and I explore the tall shelves being stocked by men in aprons.

We zip around shoppers leisurely pushing their carts. I don't even realize that John has left my side. We're all in separate aisles now, and John and I notice some very odd things about the people in the grocery store. I stand staring dumb struck at a one-legged man. "Come here, John!" I yell. No answer. I project my voice over stacks of cans of pork and beans. "You've got to come see this one-legged man!"

"No, you come here!" John shouts back to me over the Fruit Loops. "You've got to see the shortest little lady I ever did see!" John has sighted a dwarf.

"No, John, you come here! There's a man with a rolled-up pant leg." I squat down low to inspect the man's empty pant leg. "Where'd you put your leg," I ask him. He leans on his cart and says, "My leg? Why, it's at the churchyard."

Mom hears our voices and flies around the aisles with her cart. With a murderous look, she grabs me, then John by his scrawny neck, and marches us to the exit. This could be our very last trip to the grocery store.

Mom does not take us with her to the bank, but one day, she returns home from the bank with a colorful balloon. I grab it and inflate it, blowing out my cheeks in a mighty effort. John complains. He's sure Mom intended the balloon for him. When she asks me to give it to John, I cry, "but it's got my air in it!"

ON WEEKENDS, I watch fascinated as Dad winds his increasingly vast clock collection. Most run eight days without winding. Dad can smoke a Raleigh cigarette as he winds them, a task he often completes while we are at mass at St. Paul's Catholic Church, praying for him as he's asked. Dad is strong and powerful but mysterious. I know where he stands on many subjects. He does not care for Catholicism, but he likes Catholics, especially Mom. He considers himself agnostic, but he writes a poem about God, "The Sublime Architect."

Mass is fun for me. Women and girls are required to cover their heads in church, so Hannah, Mom, and I walk into the small church wearing "chapel veils," that look like lace doilies, bobby-pinned to our hair. Our Easter outfits still fit. My pearly, patent leather shoes are a bit scuffed now and squeeze my toes. Invariably, John and I are separated because he makes jokes and we can't stop giggling. Craning my neck overtop the pew, I find Mr. Keeney, my godparent, waiting to wink and smile at me.

That afternoon, Ed offers to teach John and me a new card game. We look at each other in wonder. "Are you gonna play some card games with *us?*" we ask Ed. "52 pickup," he says.

We already know go fish, concentration, and crazy eights. We can tell the reds from the blacks, the hearts from the diamonds, and the clubs from the spades. Jokers usually stay in the box; aces have *A*s; clubs have rounded clovers; spades are the other ones. We know how to deal and keep score. "One for you, one for me. Two for you, two for me." I like the control when I'm the dealer. Sometimes John says, "Let's not cheat this time."

Ed makes a show of his thick, football-playing fingers. He's so strong, he can grip the full deck with just one hand. "Isn't it my turn to deal? Tell John it's my turn to deal, Ed," I plead. But Ed still holds all the cards.

I like everything about playing cards, like when it's my turn to draw from the draw pile. I get to decide all by myself what to do with my new, private card. I sometimes show it to John. I'm learning to make important decisions that take time. Should I hold, or should I discard?

"You *sure* you want to play 52 pickup?" Ed asks.

"Of course!" we answer in unison. Our big brother takes his football-playing hand and flails all fifty-two cards to the ceiling. They explode, scattering over every nook and cranny of the room.

"Okay," he says, erupting in laughter. "Now go pick them all up!"

I start to cry. John just stares with wide eyes. Slowly, we pick up the cards.

At other times, I'm too charmed by my big brother to remember his tricks. One spring evening when I'm allowed to stay up way past bedtime, he walks in the back door dressed in his prom attire: a white, tuxedo jacket; his bow tie loosened like a Hollywood star. He picks me up and lifts me onto his shoulders. I feel like a little queen.

BY LATE JUNE, the clouds are small marshmallow puffs of goodness against the bluest Virginia skies. John and I jump around the yard, playing our own version of tag, claiming the other person is always "it." After endless stops and starts, we are breathless. John points at cloud shapes. "I see a turtle. And he's following an alligator," he says, squinting at the sun.

"I see Aladdin's lamp," I declare. A triangular cloud with a curlycue at one end, like the handle on a lantern, catches my eye. "I don't see it." John's legs are in motion again; he's run off too quickly.

Once it warms up enough and we can swim, using the doggy-paddle, and jump from the side of the community pool, Hannah, John, and I splash around like little pets let loose. Ed's in charge. But after an hour or so, we're bored. That's when Ed suggests his favorite swimming pool game: "Go down three times and come up twice." Dad and Ed are chock-full of orneriness, and we learn to recognize their tricks.

Dad arrives at the breakfast table where Mom pours him his hot coffee, which he slurps satisfyingly. After a little caffeine, he sings to us, his youngest children; we've been up since before sunrise. While Mom stands over the frying pans and turning bacon, flipping pancakes, Dad sips his coffee and studies his audience. Our freckled faces, rapt with attention, are barely above the tabletop near our waiting plates. We start giggling when Dad does his strange expressions, as if Mom has told him privately, "Entertain the kids while I'm cooking, or they'll start whining." Dad twists his lips into puckers that make us laugh even more. He changes his deep voice to a much higher pitch to enhance his songs and limericks as we snicker away. He sings the tunes in a funny voice and raises his eyebrows. His comical expressions add to the stories. He laughs too, entertained by some of the blank stares we give each other when we don't have any idea what his punch lines mean. Mom seldom stops him, but occasionally admonishes him with, "Oh, stop!"

"I had a little dog and his name was Rover; and when he died, [pause] he died all over." As Mom sets her most delicious pancakes in front of us, we can only picture poor Rover, dead all over.

DR. GEOFFREY owns Lebanon Hospital where he serves as a general practitioner. Since he performs minor surgeries, he performs the tonsillectomies on Ed, John and me. Leading up to the surgeries, John and I are told of the comforting treats we can demand afterward: all the ice cream and popsicles we want!

I awake from surgery with my throat on fire. Ed's in a room down the hall, and John's lying in a bed across the room from me. He and I wail like babies. Mom walks back and forth from my bed to John's like a frantic bed nurse, trying to comfort us, trying to get us to stop crying so our throats won't hurt so much. Some time later, after we're sitting up and quiet, Dr. Geoffrey comes by. He hands us jars that held our tonsils suspended in liquid. I don't know if it's the sight of those nasty lymph nodes or the effects of the anesthesia, but when Dr. Geoffrey suggests I take a walk with him down the hallway, I'm terribly nauseated. You'd think he might notice my pale, stricken face. He urges me to take his hand. I try to be strong; I love him like a grandfather. I walk down the hall with him, my thin frame swallowed by my hospital gown. I have the worst taste in my mouth and my throat is on fire again. When Dr. Geoffrey introduces me to the staff behind the nurses' station, I smile weakly, hoping this social visit will end quickly. Back in my room, just inside the threshold, I prove how nauseous I am.

John and Ed go home, but losing the contents of my stomach keeps me in the hospital on intravenous fluids for one more night. Once home, Mom fixes my favorite homemade pancakes, but I can't eat a bite. Everything tastes terrible and hurts my throat, even ice cream. To this day, I cannot tolerate the aftereffects of anesthesia.

ONE SUNDAY, John suggests we cut the Sunday comics out in squares and strips. "We can sell these! C'mon, Sarah, let's go see who will pay us a nickel," John says. The two of us set out to knock on doors and pawn our bounty. We extract nickels here and there from the perplexed but friendly neighbors who maybe feel sorry for the scrawny Blizzard kids from down the street.

John wakes me up often with fresh ideas about what we can get away with that day. "Hey, Sarah, I know where some matches are. Let's go catch the grass on fire." Or "Let's steal some money out of Mom's purse."

I want to remember these days as idyllic. I throw into a deep shadow my awareness that by the time he's six, John's both rebellious and secretive. He's been branded the scapegoat and consistently takes the brunt of Dad's anger, which I facilitate by tattling every time John does anything worth telling on. Occasionally, Mom makes an excuse for her baby boy. She might even throw Hannah or me under the bus to thwart Dad's accusations. John develops a closeness with his only defender. But it's clear, nevertheless, that Mom's allegiance is with her man.

BY AUGUST, we have our marching orders: "Don't you kids come back inside all day," Mom says. John and I are more than happy to comply. School will resume the following week, and we plan to make the most of daylight. In my Annie Oakley boots, I march along the Virginia Highlands woods and briers, home to wild Indians, Daniel Boone and me. My hair is pulled back in a curly ponytail. John's got his summer buzz cut as part of a yearly ritual conducted on the driveway when Dad sets John atop a Sears catalog that's atop a kitchen chair and throws a dishcloth on John's shoulders. Two minutes later, John's left with a few bristles.

"Reach in my paper sack and tell me what all Mom put in there," says John. He hoists the fishing-pole-sized branch he's found deep in the meadow. He's cute, just like Tom Sawyer. "Saltines." I munch away on my salty treat, peanut butter peeking out between the layers. "Look, she made 'em just the way I like," I say, swinging my ponytail. "Aren't you hungry?"

John lays down his stick, reaches to the bottom of his bag and takes a bite of juicy apple. "Wish she'd put some of that Dentyne gum in there," he says. I saw him pinch Dentyne from Mom's pocketbook yesterday afternoon when we were supposed to be napping. I'm telling on him when we get home. Last time he peed outside, I tattled, and he got a spanking.

After lunch, we head over to the field where the cows are enclosed by a big wire fence. Up ahead, the Ott and Murphy boys lay on a flattened refrigerator box, their dirty fingernails clinging to their dog-eared cardboard sled. With each run on their slippery slope, they mash down thick brush. Their blue jeans are slick with shiny, red clay. John tosses his stick and turns to pee in the weeds. "Sarah, this time don't tell on me," he says. He doesn't know what all I've saved in my tattle box, like coins in my piggy bank.

"C'mon, let's go. I'll give you a hand up Farmer Blankenship's hill," John says. "I want to see the horns on that bull." He spits into his dirty palms and grabs his stick. I reach up for the stick, but John grabs my hand to help me up the incline. We approach the fence where the beasts beyond the hot wired fence protest our presence with rotund moos. I smell steamy cow patties, just like the ones so perfectly placed last Christmas Eve on our snow-covered lawn. Dad woke us up Christmas morning, smiling mischievously and declaring, "Come look! Santa and all of his reindeer have been right here! See? Rudolph pooped in the yard!"

John and I lose track of time in the meadow, chasing the weight-less dandelion seeds. We whistle them away and watch them float like fairies across rabbit holes. Dusk falls over a cool creek bed shadowing wiggly minnows that zigzag away from our cupped hands. Mom calls out, "Biscuits 'r ready!" Our hearts race us home.

In our cozy three-bedroom home, one room leads to the next, like an open maze. Knotty pine wraps like wainscoting around the central-ized kitchen. The round, oak table nestles among shuttered windows that look out onto our driveway. The adjacent living room, generally thought of as Mom and Dad's room, is the scene of their nightly card game. We learn to play duplicate solitaire by standing next to Mom and watching her every move against Dad.

I pick up on things that are said and things that aren't. I have better instincts than John: I know how to stay out of the way, when to insert some clever remark to get a laugh. John isn't as quick. He sets Dad off too easily. He's the object of Dad's wrath when we play tug-of-war over a toy or jump on the furniture. When Dad walks out to get another sharp switch from a bush, I expect it is the back of John's legs that will sting the most.

IT'S A CRISP FRIDAY NIGHT after the Lebanon High School football game. Ed plays center. A deep snow has descended. Postgame, bundled in woolen scarves and heavy coats, everyone gathers around the bon-fire that the young men have built. Ed and his friends huddle shoulder to shoulder in their letter jackets and stoke the flames with long sticks. Just below the bonfire site is a long, steep, narrow back road—the toboggan run.

One memorable winter's night, past my bedtime, when the snow was knee-high, I beg Ed to let me lie atop his back on the long toboggan. He agrees, but he issues strict orders. "When I say 'ready', you hold on tight!" His voice competes with the whistle in the wind and the crackle of the bonfire. I grab his shoulders with all my might. We take off and frigid air blasts my face. In seconds, we reach the bottom where the road levels. I'm hooked. "Let's do it again!"

Ed jumps up, grabs the lead rope from deep in the snow, and realigns the front of the toboggan. I adjust quickly to a seated position as Ed turns me around to begin the steep climb. My face is set to the crowd on the hill above us as my hero hauls me up. Sarah means "princess" and I feel as regal as my name.

FROM THE OUTSIDE, we look like a model family. Dad favors me. People say I look like him. "She has her dad's eyes; it's as if he had Sarah himself," they say. He'll scoop me up next to him on the couch, and I'll snuggle with my head on his chest, admiring his Masonic ring—the one he wears on his wedding finger—as he twists and turns it so I can see it from all angles. I stay put while he and Mom play cards. I feel safe against his chest, his soft flannel shirt, his manliness. But after another drink, he or Mom says, "Scoot," or I just know it's time to leave. Already, though just a child, I can sense when Mom and Dad are off-limits. I can gauge Dad's inebriation on his walk from the kitchen back to the living room. When his gait grows unsure, his bottom lip swells and his drunken voice becomes demanding. "Never trust a man who can't hold his liquor!" is one of his favorite orations.

Mom and Dad take Hannah, John, and me to Kentucky to visit the Greens. Our parents get drunk with the Greens. There's nothing for us kids to do. Stella and Matthew have a miniature dachshund that growls ferociously and snaps at us. Hannah, John, and I make ourselves scarce.

Hannah has brought a book with her. She disappears to read. Two neighbor boys wearing T-shirts and jeans walk by. They look close to John's age. They motion for John to join them. I follow as they play Tarzan—swing from tree branches and show off for each other. I've never been agile, so I keep my distance. When they descend from their jungle, they take off running. I run to keep up. They stop at the top of a ten-foot wall next to a driveway. One of the boys yells and jumps. The second boy does the same, then John. They each land with their knees bent, but jump up immediately and run off again, screaming "Charge!" One of the boys watches me. I think he expects me to follow. It doesn't look so hard. I jump. When I land, I turn my ankle. I'm in excruciating pain but try not to cry as I hobble to Matthew and Stella's house where the four drunk adults are in Stella's kitchen.

Mom takes a look at my injured ankle, now twice its normal size. I hear the word X-ray followed by "Issss barely a spain." The radio's set to country music. Dad reaches down, takes my hand, and tries to pull me up. My ankle throbs. Dad wants to dance with me. The four adults are laughing. I manage to stand up. Dad grabs me in a waltz. He's going to dip me the way he dips Mom in the TV room on Saturday nights. He doesn't make two steps when I break down in sobs from the searing pain. Mom urges Dad to unhand me. She gets a bag of ice.

I remember some lines from a poem by Theodore Roethke, about a boy dancing with his father, and I imagine it's about me: "The whiskey on your breath could make a small boy dizzy," and "We romped until the pans slid from the kitchen shelf." So I'm not the only one with parents who are drunk all the time.

Stella finds an ace bandage, but wrapping that swollen joint is agonizing. We don't spend the night. On the way home, we stop in Dunbar, where Granny lives now in a smaller house than the one she had in Green Bank.

On one of our other visits to Kentucky, when I'm seven, Mom and Stella run out for cigarettes and take me with them. Neither is sober enough to drive. I stand on the front seat between them, my head touching the ceiling. It's 1965. No seat belts. Stella drives. Traffic thickens and she suddenly slams on the brakes. Mom reaches for me but can't prevent my pitch forward. My forehead hits the windshield. I'm stunned but not hurt. "Don't tell your dad about this," Mom says. "Yeah, Sweetie, don't say anything to anyone," Stella says.

Cape Cod Summers

IN THE SAME WAY WE ANTICIPATE CHRISTMAS, we look forward to an annual two-week sojourn away from our real world to New England's idyllic Cape Cod shores. This is our reward for all of Dad's hard work: our departure from the Virginia Highlands to a vacation where there are no creepy neighbors waiting to pull down our pants, only strangers with funny accents who basically stick to themselves. I can find Cape Cod's curved hook on any map, and I want to be there.

Our green Ford Galaxie 500 four-door is packed the night before we depart and, until I can hold my eyes open no longer, I lie in bed staring at the neat stack of travel clothes that Mom has placed on my nightstand. In the wee hours, while it's still dark outside, Mom wiggles my shoulder. Her voice is soft, "Sarah, c'mon."

"Time to leave?" I ask. I hear one of Dad's cuckoo birds chiming four times. Mom holds a pair of shorts to my toes, and I blindly step into them. They're my new ones with the elastic waist. Next comes the T-shirt.

"Go use the bathroom," she says. "Then get in the car." We're loaded into the back seat. Ed, Hannah, John, and me. I sit up in the back seat until my siblings settle in. Our parents finish packing the car; whatever doesn't fit is strapped to the roof. Off we go, filled to capacity. As we leave Lebanon Manor, Ed stretches flat in the back seat. Hannah, John and I sit on top of his back, his butt, and his legs. Our shoulders become a sibling's headrest. We nod off, a stack of interconnected octopuses, appendages woven together, entwined as our lives will always be. What a welcome divergence awaits us: instead of the Virginia Highlands' hard, red clay, there will be fine, warm sand and warm ocean breezes, lighthouses, starfish, the freshest seafood, and days of exploration. We nod off.

Around five-thirty, we wake to the barest hint of sunrise. I search the horizon in silence, my heart beating to the rhythm and hum of the car's engine. The Pennsylvania farmland is one continuous landscape until we approach the outskirts of New York City.

Family-vacation cars like ours and semitrucks whiz past until Dad joins them in the left-hand lane. We pass them, and then they pass us. For a few seconds we're side-by-side on the smooth, black asphalt highway, apparently moving towards a traffic jam. Dad slams on the brakes. We all jerk a bit and stare at the spectacle: for miles ahead, no cars are moving. We roll our windows down. We watch kids in the next car over stick their bare feet out their windows. Mom won't allow us to do the same. It looks rude, she says. But we like the fresh air; Mom and Dad have been chain-smoking in the closed-up car.

Once we pick up speed again, the windows go up, and the car fills again with cigarette smoke. Occasionally, Dad slows down on back roads. Someone farts and we roll down windows. We slip an arm out, allow our hands to ride the wave of the oncoming wind. When Dad passes a trucker, we pump our forearms and hands. The bearded fellow in the seat high above us honks, which makes us giddy with laughter. Inside tunnels, dad honks. Going down hills, he speeds up, creating the sensation of a carnival ride.

WE MAKE UP GAMES using the alphabet. We sing songs we write on the spot. When we see a water tower, John and I name it "Timmy." We make up a song called "Timmy the Water Tower." Ed likes to reach outside his window and pound on the roof. When I ask, "What was that?" he says, "Santa Claus!" I believe him.

Mom advocates for us when we need a bathroom break, a need that Dad tends to ignore. We're relieved when Dad's backside gets numb or the gas gauge is on *E*. We learn to hold it until we can't any longer. Dad finally stops, practically side-swiping a guardrail. If there's no restroom in sight, we girls race for a place to squat. Mom's always a few yards ahead of us sunk in grassy tufts. Before we climb back in the car, someone empties the overflowing ashtray.

After hours and hours, we revert to the ways of kids who have been in a car for hours and hours. "He's touching me!" "How much longer?"

Dad relies on Mom to navigate. Invariably, they start fussing. Dad rides the left-hand lane and misses an exit. Dad's leg cramps from keeping the pedal to the metal. He's also rubbing his forehead in frustration. There are miles to go. Does he need a drink other than coffee or ice water? Mom warns him repeatedly to "Slow down! Didn't you see that cop car?" The loud siren makes my heart jump into my throat! Dad pulls over, and the officer looks in the window at our freckly faces. He tells Dad to step outside. We hear Dad say, "Just keeping up with the traffic, officer." We crouch down in our seats. Will Dad go to jail? But we're soon on our way.

It's quiet in the car. Dad's been humbled. Time after time, his speeding costs him. Every summer, he's issued a speeding ticket coming and going. With Dad's tail between his legs, Mom's voice turns sympathetic. "Some ice water?" She pours him a drink. By the time we stop at a roadside rest area for our main meal, the tension is gone. We enjoy a quick, classic picnic: sandwiches, chips, fruit, and cookies, plus Dad's favorite, chocolate Heath bars.

It's the pre-seatbelt era. I fold myself up like a fetus on the floorboard. But when our parents alert us to a remarkable sight—a power plant like Dad's, an expansive bridge over the Hudson River, or a tunnel carved out of a mountain—I scramble for a window.

Once in a while, I'm allowed to climb into the front seat between my parents, usually after Mom's finished her cigarette and the two adults are done with coffee. I love the scent of the fresh-perked stimulant and watching Mom tip the thermos into their waiting containers. Dad holds his thermos cup precariously with one overgrown forefinger and sips as if it's an elixir.

When I plop down between them, Dad grins at me, pats my knee, and says, "Hi, Bud." I believe I'm his favorite. Mom hands me a pen and a scratch pad so I can practice my letters. I write clumsily, mostly backwards, but the activity puts pause to my question, "How much longer?" Mom and Dad tell us that if they had a quarter for every time one of us asks that question, they could afford a room for a night.

Mom persuades Dad to pull into a gas station so we can use the bathroom. When we return, Dad asks how we did. Hannah says, "I did number one!" John says, "I did number two!" I tell him, "I did number three." Mom looks at me and I explain. "Number one and two both."

JUST AFTER SUNRISE, after a full day in the car, we arrive at our little three-bedroom cottage along a quiet street nestled in tall pine trees. Our fourteen-day vacation spreads out before us like a welcome mat, in strange and mysterious Dennis Port, Massachusetts. We fall asleep on the single beds in the cottage. Once the weariness wears off, we explore. I breathe in the heavy, pine scent and taste the salty air. I listen to ocean waves crashing a few hundred yards away.

The sea—its colors, shape, and power, the texture it draws on the sandy beach—stops me in my tracks. The stark, gray, powerful ocean is one zillion times bigger than at Hungry Mother State Park. Mom and Dad stand nearby, quietly waiting to see our reaction. Wind mixed with salt blows my hair straight behind my head, and I can taste its saltiness on my lips. The air is cool, and we're glad Mom insisted we wear our Cape Cod sweat shirts. The grains of sand between my toes are so different from Virginia's red clay dirt. Dunes rise in countless mounds behind us, and the awesome sea stretches out as far as we can see underneath a light blue, cloudless sky. Like a perpetually changing painting, its artistic movement inspires many questions.

Are the distant waves creating the wind, or is the wind creating them? Why does the wind blow sideways here, against my face? Why are some waves foamy? Others clap against the shoreline, spread out, then buckle back under. Why do waves come crashing ashore only to be dragged back out to sea? Further out are their gigantic white-capped brothers and sisters, all with a rhythm I'm trying to grasp. All of it begs me: be a witness.

While Mom and Dad unpack, Ed takes Hannah, John, and me along a carpet of coarse sand mixed with sticky pine needles that toughen our bare feet. On the beach, we climb over rock jetties that extend out into the ocean every hundred feet. Exotic creatures—live starfish—cling to the undersides of warm, granite boulders covered with black barnacles.

After days on end of sandcastle-building and wave-jumping, Ed wields a shovel for the laborious task of hole-digging. Bare chested and muscular, he works on his tan as John or I are ceremoniously inserted into deep holes. "Get in," Ed says. Then, he covers us up to our shoulders with sand. When he's done, we're just creepy kid heads dotting the beach.

"Look, Dad!" the heads yell. He laughs at our bizarre spectacle. Dad is on one of three missions: by day, to see how many fish he can catch off one of the rock jetties; by afternoon, how many clocks or boxes of parts he can talk local antique shop owners out of; and by night, how much he can drink.

THE PROPRIETORS OF THE LOCAL ANTIQUE SHOPS, where we browse for hours, welcome our parents. Dad dickers with each one over old, run-down clocks, or, better yet, clock parts—loose hands and clock faces, mostly with Roman numerals. We wander, and Mom gravitates toward old china pieces, glassware, and the occasional wooden duck decoy.

I'm drawn to a female mannequin propped up on a staircase landing and outfitted in a loose dress and a dusty, felt hat that hides one eye. I study a cast-off baby doll dressed in a moth-eaten shift. The doll sits in a window looking like something that might have been owned by a little girl who plastered a lonely expression on its face before the girl died.

We walk barefoot to the local beach market. Friendly folk who run the seasonal grocery would never dream of posting a sign like, "No Shoes, No Shirt, No Service." We come in with sticky pine tar and sand between our bare toes, and nickels in hand for our favorite penny candy, Atomic Fire Balls. We like the locals' funny accents: "Park your car" sounds like "Pack ya ka."

John is on his best behavior. The next-door neighbors, who every year rent the same cottage the same weeks as we do, bring their two children. They are close to our age—John and me. We chase each other around the property. Mom takes pictures of us blowing bubbles from the wands that we've dipped in bubble liquid then hold to our pursed lips. Or we traipse back beyond the roadside grocery to the great Atlantic Ocean.

We grow ravenous during our days at the shore and develop a taste for the fresh scallops and lobster meat at the Wee Packet restaurant in Dennis Port. On rainy days, our parents drive us to weathered lighthouses where we climb spiral staircases.

WE WATCH WAVES BUILD until they crash ashore again and again. Dad picks up an empty conch shell larger than his hand and holds it up like treasured bounty—no cracks or chips. I expect him to place it in his bucket. Instead, he sets the bucket down next to his fishing pole and fastens the shell to his ear like a telephone. "Let me hear!" I reach for the shell. He hands it to me. "Put it tight to your ear. You'll hear the ocean." I'm amazed! My brother reaches for it. I want him to hear it too. We've never seen this playful, relaxed side of our hard-working dad.

A hefty wind blows across the water, against my face, and deposits fresh sand around my ankles. When a wave creates a water pool, my bare feet start to sink. I jump out, jump up, again and again, in harmony with the waves. The wind, or gravity, or some mysterious force folds them over and under, then drags them back to sea. Dad moves on, combing the beach for trinkets. He finds scallop and mussel shells and puts them in his bucket collection. I follow him, putting my bare feet in the footprints he's left behind.

I taste more salt on my lips and spy Cape Cod's welcoming dunes and sea grass. I'm so thankful to Dad for expanding my world as well as my vocabulary. I catch up to him climbing the jetties. Dozens of them, extending out into the ocean, are lined up as far as I can see. We kids climb aboard as Dad stops to retrieve a starfish; he puts it into his bucket and shows us how they cling to the undersides of our granite jungle-gym, the jetty. "Ouch!" I say, pointing to something sharp, the same color as the rocks.

"Barnacles," he says. "Beware of them." He teaches us about low tides and high tides. "Are the tides medium too?" I ask. Dad chuckles, pats me on the head. "Nope, just high or low, depending on the time of day." While Dad casts his fishing line out over the ocean, we kids race back to shore, to build a sandcastle. We collect more shells for Dad.

Back at the cottage, he hands us a nickel, and we trek down to the roadside grocery store for penny candy. After supper, we follow his tracks back down to the beach, sidling up next to him but dwarfed by his broad shoulders as he stares toward the distant signals coming from a lighthouse far offshore. When he was in the navy, he was trained in Morse code. When he decodes the flashing lights it's like he knows another language. Dad gets a faraway look in his eyes when he gazes out beyond the horizon line where I assume heaven is. It makes me feel very small but not insignificant at all.

"High tide's rolling in," he says. He recites a line from some ancient mariner poem. In Cape Cod, my spiritual formation takes hold naturally. I'm convinced there is a God who must've created the ocean, the sand, and all this natural beauty. And He made sure Dad brought us here to see it.

Even on Cape Cod, though, we get on Dad's nerves. When we argue and fuss over whose suitcase the huge conch shell will travel home in, Dad might grin, go easy on us, or use one of his favorite sayings, "Straighten up and fly right." He has a way of redirecting our energy. I'm blissfully happy that so many more days lie ahead. I discover that two adults and four kids can make it all the way to Cape Cod, Massachusetts, and still like each other.

THE VERY NEXT SUMMER, we repeat the rituals. Only this time, we kids become victims of a monster worse than the sea.

"Here's today's tide report," Mom tells Dad. Keeping track of tides has become a game to our parents, like keeping track of their beloved Cincinnati Reds' standings in the league or watching the stock market. For devoted fishermen like Dad, twelve hours is a long time to wait. I guess that's how much time there is between tides, assuming there are only two tides per day, low and high. I don't want to keep asking questions. Having lived with Dad's clocks chiming every hour on the hour and, for some, also on the quarter hour and half hour, I figure tides follow suit.

For these two weeks, we've run barefoot over pine needles and eaten delicate fresh scallops and lobsters; then, too soon, it'll be time to go home. Today, though, it's stormy. Mom and Dad play hand after hand of cards. I ignore them. When Dad begins slurring his words and hiccupping, I mind my own business until Dad says, "Jis wan more try. Gotta kesh the big one." He wants to go fishing, but he's far too drunk. It's almost dark. It's high tide. But he's made up his mind.

Perhaps if we take no notice of him, he'll have another drink, forget about it, and pass out. But as the sun sets, Dad only gets louder. He brags about his impending catch. Hannah, John, and I are playing a board game. I can't gauge their feelings, but I'm gripped with fear. We look at each other wide-eyed and dump the letters from the Scrabble game back into the box. Dad puts on his Top-Sider shoes. "Cod's bitin' ride now, I tell you!" he bellows.

During low tide, when the water's calmer, Dad would climb the jetties to fish. But in these rough conditions? In the dark? But there's no stopping him. He grabs his fishing gear. "You kids go with him," says Mom, who's also loaded by now. None of us has the nerve to ask what happens if he falls off the jetty onto the rocks. John grins and pulls a shiny quarter out of his pocket. "Let's flip for who gets to carry the flashlight!" he says.

Maybe getting out of this stifling cottage will be all right. Maybe, while Dad fishes, we can watch the moon reflect off the water, gather more shells. We might catch a glimpse of sand crabs peeking out from under their mounds.

DAD STAGGERS OUTDOORS, lets the screen door slam, and steadies himself. We can't rely on him to lead the way so we run ahead. John, with his Eveready, races Hannah and me. We pass five or six identical cottages, cross the last street, and we're at the path to the surf. We have the street to ourselves. Normal families are indoors for the night. We spread out, moving much more quickly than Dad. For a few moments we almost forget how waxed he is. The air feels breezy. We swing our arms in a wordless cadence. Our flip-flops smack like gum against the pavement as we speed-walk.

My eyes adjust to the night, softly lit by low-wattage lamps. At the end of our road, we wait for Dad. My brother shines his light on him as he zigzags, mumbling. Dad's a sight. His baggy, short pants are held up by a weathered rope belt he made himself. His favorite plaid, short-sleeved shirt, the one Mom bought him because it has a chest pocket for his cigarettes and lighter, hangs over his pants. His fishing hat sits tilted on his head. His worn-out tennis shoes are stained by sand and salt water. He carries his trusty metal tackle box in one hand; in the other is a long pole with a sharp, curvy hook dangling from its end. The streetlights illuminate all six foot three, two hundred pounds of him, as he lurches past us and crosses the street. We fall in behind him, marching single file like overgrown ducklings following our drunken drake.

The surface of the path is a coarse rug of pine needles and crunchy cone fragments. I know better than to kick off my sandals just yet, but a sticky needle covered with sand works its way between my flip-flop and big toe. I stop to remove it, but my ponytail ends up across my eyes. I wait for the howling wind to calm. Sand makes its way onto my lips.

Tall reeds narrow the way. Dad lists to the right like a polka dancer with no partner to swing. My brother stifles a giggle. Dad catches himself and lifts his size 12s onto solid sand. We're on the beach. I kick off my flip-flops.

We walk on under a veiled moon that casts an eerie glow in the darkening sky. I glance back to the spot where I left my flip-flops, but I can't see them. Hannah and John spread out, giving Dad a wide berth. He clomps over to the rock jetties. I want the assurance of a grown-up presence, but there's none. I swallow hard.

DAD CLIMBS UP ON THE FIRST BIG BOULDER and almost drops his tackle box. The hooks, bobbers, and sinkers within toss about and rattle. He falters, regains his balance and grasps the box handle more firmly. He zigzags, teeters, and makes his way down the jagged trail of glistening rocks.

I perch on the fifth big rock and sit with legs crossed. Pocks in the boulders beneath my folded legs cradle puddles of warm sea water. Despite the cool wind, they've stored the day's earlier warmth. I'm surrounded by narrow openings and deep crevices where live things cling to rocks. I envision octopus tendrils appearing like sea monsters between every nook and cranny, grabbing each of us with slimy suction-cupped arms and drowning us. I hope John doesn't ask me to spy on sea urchins or go crabbing or shelling. If Hannah wants to point out the stars and find constellations, I'll wave her off and tell her I can't pay attention.

I search the distant rocks for Dad's silhouette. I make out his shape close to the end of the jetty. He lifts his leg in an awkward balance on the obstacle course created by the rugged rocks. The pounding surf over-tops the jetty's end, drenching Dad to his waist. I hyperventilate. I'm too petrified to breathe normally. I beg the crashing waves not to take him.

Should I yell, "Dad, look out!" or signal for help? What if the next surge takes him under? My breath catches in my throat when I see him upright, still wearing his hat. Maybe now he'll bait that hook, cast his line, catch a cod, and end this nightmare. Hannah has hoisted herself onto a rock. Behind me, she hums a tune. John is searching the barna-cled rocks with his Eveready. I can tell by the flicker that his batteries are low.

Dad's on the jetty's tip now. Wave after wave crashes around him. He raises his fishing rod, casts the line, wobbles, then braces himself, feet apart, pees, and spits. Miles away, a lighthouse flashes. If any of us fall from these boulders, there will be no SOS. Dad straddles two boul-ders in a wide stance. As the waves break, he jumps a bit, then his feet come back together. The crashing waters band together like demon sea monsters laughing at him and taunting. He's their catch. They splash their salt up to his swollen lip. Another wave breaks against his legs. I can barely see him. When the splash subsides, he's gone! Our drunken patriarch has jumped into the Atlantic Ocean. I can see that he has something huge on his line—perhaps the largest catch of the summer, the year, ever—and he's not about to let go. He's waited his entire life for such a fish. In water up to his chest, he holds on to the pole. The creature pulls the line hard, straight and level with the waves. I fear it will win. But Dad holds on and keeps his whiskey-soaked eyes on the prize. The ocean and the catch-of-his-life demand he struggle. He tugs. He walks backwards into shallower water, lifts his long legs out of danger, reels in the line, and hops backwards over the diminishing waves.

The walk back is bittersweet. I'm barefoot, I've aged a few years, but Dad is alive. The demon-prize is still wiggling, but barely. It's almost dead. Dad isn't, though he's soaked head to toe. I'm calmer now. My feet are toughening up, and so am I.

Mom is waiting at the screen door with a camera. She captures Dad laughing in victory over his thirty-inch trophy. Over the years, his triumph becomes legend. He reviews the photograph again and again and retells from his point of view the story of how he drank all day and then caught the biggest fish ever. Hannah, John, and I keep our version to ourselves.

OUR PARENTS PACK THE CAR and strap a newly acquired grandfather clock to the top of the station wagon. On the drive home, I hear Dad snicker to himself. I imagine he's reliving his triumphal moments. In the back seat, I roll my eyes. Why is it that Dad claims he drinks because his job at the plant is so stressful, yet a two-week vacation becomes a drunk fest? We kids are more exhausted than usual on that trip home. I am shell-shocked.

II

Shift in Gears

I LOVE MRS. O'CONNOR, our neighbor and my kindergarten and first grade teacher, as much as I love my own mother. Mrs. O'Connor favors me. Since I read well, she asks me to help her. "Sarah, I need you to come sit in my chair while I walk the bus students down the hallway. You read to the class." I'm thrilled to be her little leader. My classmates sit in a circle in front of me, all eyes on my book. I hold the book open and turn it around, just like Mrs. O'Connor did, so the children can all see the pictures.

Happy at school, when I overhear news of Dad's transfer, I'm crestfallen. Dad and Ed are arguing, and it's getting loud in the living room. In my bedroom refuge, I sob uncontrollably. If Dad hears me, he'll see the tears as my childish protest to his promotion. I don't want him raising his voice at me. I hide in the closet.

Our dog, Fritzy, barely lifts his ear when I unfold the louvered doors. He's in his favorite spot, smack-dab in the middle of Granny's braided rug that covers the hardwood floor between the two beds. I kick my cowgirl boots aside and plop down; I guide the bifold doors closed in front of me. My shoulders are shaking from crying, and I pull my knees up to my chin. I let it all out. And, even though my vision blurs, when I squint, I can see through the doors' narrow slats.

Two angry voices resound down the hallway. Ed doesn't want to move during his senior year of high school. Who can blame him? He has at least one pretty girlfriend, maybe two, and his best friends, Butch and Jack. Who'll organize their sledding parties and bonfires?

My other siblings are nowhere in sight. Dad has announced in no uncertain terms that the new job is a done deal. We're moving to West Virginia. Surely not Pocahontas County, I hope. The only thing there besides Granny is the radio observatory and the farm.

I listen to Dad and Ed go head to head. Mom sits off to the side in her rocking chair—legs crossed, her unfiltered Camel in one hand, the other arm folded across her lap—saying nothing. Maybe, in her mind, she's already rearranging the furniture. I wonder if Hannah and John want to move.

Everything quiets when, suddenly, I hear Dad's hard breath enter my room, fueled by cigarettes and bourbon. From where I cower, I can see his plaid flannel shirt in horizontal stripes, like the fabric-strips Granny keeps precut in a sack for making quilts. When he opens the folding doors, he points his thick finger at me.

"We're moving! That's all there is to it. Now, straighten up!" His voice is so loud, Fritzy rushes out. I hate it when Dad thinks he's the judge of everything. I'm on Ed's side. But I don't say a word. I just wipe my eyes with my shirttail. I wipe my nose too, get up out of the closet and plop down on my bed. I grab my reader. I turn the pages of *Dick and Jane*, not really reading. How can we just leave? There's nobody else in Lebanon who can repair the town bell-tower clock inside the courthouse. Dad's a local hero for the work he's done on the gigantic works, getting the gears all in sync. We pass the landmark often, reminded of the sacrifice Dad made climbing up the skinny stairs inside the tower. He said he was afraid his eardrums would burst when he had to check the chimes, sixty feet in the air. But boxes get filled and loaded onto the Mayflower moving van.

IT'S JANUARY 1966 and in a blinding snowstorm when we pull into the Woodsdale neighborhood in Wheeling, a city in the "northern panhandle" of West Virginia.

I'm suddenly ecstatic. A blizzard for the Blizzards! A snowstorm has hit our new town the minute the movers begin to unload our furnishings. The Mayflower workers persevere, despite the low visibility. I'm glad to be out of the car. So, this is it!

On our corner lot sits a tall, hunter green, cedar-shake home. Solid, front-porch steps are wooden and painted a soft gray. While Mom directs the movers, Hannah and I run in to the house and go upstairs to investigate. She and I will share a room at the top of the stairs; John's room is all the way in the back of the upstairs around the bend from the attic door. He has his own narrow, wooden, private staircase with high treads that lead directly into the kitchen. Ed will have a bed in the little room off the landing.

Mom and Dad have a large bedroom replete with a cozy alcove for their bed. Hannah and I run downstairs to find Mom. "Can we have that big bedroom with the archway where the bed goes?"

"No," she says. "I already told you where your room will be. And that archway is called an alcove." In our parent's room, we locate a new push-button telephone next to the space for Mom and Dad's bed. In Lebanon, we had a rotary dial.

Two weeks after moving, we notice something missing. "Where's Fritzy?"

"He's on a farm in Virginia. He never would have survived here." We start whining, thinking Mom has pulled a fast one. "Don't give me that," she says. "You're just now noticing he's gone."

OUR RELOCATION from southwestern Virginia to northern West Virginia reveals newness in every direction. Just outside the front-room window is a busy street with around-the-clock bus traffic. The city buses fart gray smoke and lurch forward after each bus stop, one right in front of our house, several times a day. Their side panels advertise for

"Elby's Big Boy Family Restaurant" and other local businesses. A steady stream of cars turn onto our street from Bethany Pike (Route 88). No longer do we inhabit the sloping hills of the Virginia Highlands, laid out in every direction as far as you can see. Wheeling, West Virginia, is a bustling metropolis.

We kids can barely sit still on our first ride downtown. The Cathedral of St. Joseph anchors a centuries-old city block. It might as well be the Sistine Chapel. There are three beautiful theaters: The Capitol Music Hall stages live performances and is home to the "Jamboree USA" live radio show. The Court and the Victoria are movie theaters. The Centre Market is so historic, it's where townspeople have been coming to sell their wares since the 1850s.

Wheeling has two welcoming city parks. Oglebay is located only a few miles uphill on Route 88. Wheeling Park is not too far in the other direction, past the beautiful mansions along historic Route 40, once an old trail for settlers moving west, now called National Road. Both parks sport recreational lakes, playgrounds, swimming pools, stately pavilions—one with an ice-skating rink—and shelters where large, family reunions and school field trips take place in the summer.

Dad seems to enjoy his new job, though he has a thirty-to-forty-minute commute. We're enrolled in nearby Woodsdale Elementary public school, and Mom puts us on a waiting list for St. Michael's Catholic school, which is taking no new students until fall. We attend catechism classes at St. Mike's after school on certain days in preparation for receiving the sacraments.

The move, with the new surroundings and people sporting northern accents that sound to me as proper as the Queen's English, has set the tone for us to be educated and raised in a lively, urban environment.

Our new northern home lacks nothing. Mom manages to fill the rooms with furniture. We even have a small TV room. A little creek runs beside the house just past a long alleyway. In winter, the creek freezes over, and branches and sticks poke hazards through the ice, which prevents ice-skating. Nevertheless, we don our new skates and try. In spring, the shallow water has a nice flow. Up the sides of the bank are some green scrub plants, all surrounded by a low, cement retaining wall. From our perch on the corner, I can smell the earthiness of the nearby creek sediment washed down from the hills after a good West Virginia rain.

We adjust quickly to our new surroundings, even to our Catholic church, so dramatically different from the small, country congregation of St. Paul's where we'd been baptized and where parishioners met in a small trailer in the Virginia Highlands. The order of the mass is the same everywhere. Communicants slowly make their way up front to the priest and stick out their tongues to receive the Eucharist. Another minister assists in dipping a chalice to the communicants' lips. Rituals of the mass are second nature for me. I know when to make the sign of the cross, genuflect, stand, sit, and kneel for various prayers.

I thumb through the hymnal as the priest or the lector stands to read from, mostly, the New Testament. I am quietly reverent even when I'm bored with the readings. I view God as someone—something— unexplainable, maybe like a giant hanging out in the sky, mysteriously causing the tides in Cape Cod and orchestrating our lives. It's simple: I love Him, and He loves me.

DAD'S VERY PROUD to be back in his native West Virginia after a seven-year sidetrack to Russell County, Virginia. He's proud of his Blizzard heritage and must feel he's come home. He becomes a fan of the Pittsburgh Pirates, especially when they play the rival Cincinnati Reds, the team Mom favors. Reds fans are sprinkled throughout the southwestern part of the state and Mom has followed them since she was a girl in Huntington. Our parents like to wager on whose team will win. Mom and Dad flirt during the games, so it's obvious the winner will get special favors. My parents can make a friendly competition out of just about anything. Dad also likes to dance with Mom in our little TV room when the *Lawrence Welk Show* plays their favorite dance tunes on Saturday nights. Mom knows one of the band members from when she used to sing in a chorus at Huntington High School. She points him out when the camera pans over the musicians. It amazes me that Mom knows someone on TV.

Part of me is content witnessing how in love our parents seem to be. In that little TV room, barely big enough for the oversized chair, ottoman, and love seat, Dad deftly and dramatically dips Mom on the dance floor at just the right time in their two-step. That's enough to send me skedaddling upstairs to my room to read a comic book.

Dad joins a bowling league with his coworkers, but his league play doesn't last long. Once Dad pulls in to the driveway after work, he seldom leaves the house again. He settles in to a routine. He drinks, smokes, plays cards, admires Mom's cooking, occasionally squeezes her buttocks, and, on Sundays, winds his vast clock collection.

Sometimes, Dad reads a book or writes poetry. He has a knack for writing poems and clever limericks. "When life seems bitter as gall, and you contemplate ending it all, don't be a jerk. Don't go berserk. Don't stand there and bawl, call Paul." Rosemary, Molly, and Ed present him with an anthology of his best writings and title it after his favorite punch line: "And There I Sat with My Piccolo." He has tears in his eyes when he opens that Christmas gift.

ONE EVENING, Dad asks me if I want to earn two quarters for shining the heavy, black, work shoes that are one of the most important tools of his trade. I feel grown-up when he entrusts this task to me, a scrawny kid. He shows me how to hold them. One shoe covers my hand and arm up to my elbow. As I apply the thick polish, it leaves stubborn streaks on my arm.

"Rub the black tar on liberally, all over," he says, "even on the sides of the soles. And work over newspaper, spread out on the floor, so you won't leave stains." I do just as he instructs. The shoes have to dry for fifteen minutes. When I check on their progress, the shiny tar has turned dull. I place each one back on my arm and hold it up to my face. With my other hand, I take the shoe brush, which Mom purchased from the same Fuller Brush man who sells Mom her hairbrushes. The polish smells like a mix of paint and boys' locker room, only more manly. I'd seen a professional shoe-shine person on TV. I knew where the term *spit-shine* came from. You can use your saliva to really get the luster going. But my mouth is closed tight as I concentrate.

Back and forth, I brush until the magic happens. The faster I stroke, the shinier the shoes become. I learn technique, and with the fifty cents I earn I'll soon have enough change to go to the Minute Market for candy. The sound of the coins tinkling into my piggy bank can't compare to the thrill I get seeing Dad's face light up when I return his shoes for inspection. The people-pleaser in me lives for his approval. "Good job!" he says.

MOM JOINS THE NEWCOMER'S CLUB and plays bridge now and then; but socializing isn't her thing. She develops a predictable routine: frequent, rather than weekly, trips to the grocery store, which includes chats with the Kroger check-out ladies. She drives to south Wheeling for fresh produce from Jebbia's. As a treat, she brings home melt-in-your-mouth donuts from Greens. And for meatless Fridays, she sometimes brings Coleman's delicious fish sandwiches. She runs errands, washes and irons clothes, and off and on catches up on an afternoon soap opera or game show.

Mom's hands are seldom idle. She collects the green stamps that are awarded for grocery purchases, glues them in a paperback book that— once full—is redeemable for household items such as plastic mixing bowls or a set of steak knives. A child of the Great Depression, Mom can recall the Christmas that she and her sister shared a doll. That was their gift. Now, she and Dad know where every dime goes. Mom wears the same clothes year after year, season after season: a thin cardigan, sensible loafers, two A-line skirts, one pair of plaid wool slacks. One light gray overcoat goes with everything that hangs in the closet. When, over the years, she gains weight, she orders a few new things from the Sears catalog. She makes grocery lists on the flap of envelopes she saves after opening the mail. In the pocket of her one apron, she keeps a tissue that she reuses through the day—or the week. Dad's the same. A few flannel shirts with breast pockets and khaki pants suit him just fine.

IF MOM DOESN'T HAVE A CIGARETTE burning in the ashtray next to where she knits, I invade her space and watch her draw yarn from a skein and knit a few rows of an afghan. Or I study her as she sews a hem; her nimble fingers and eagle-eye deftly threading the needle on the very first try.

Mom's not a housecleaner. She vacuums from time to time and clears clutter, but she doesn't dust. She empties ashtrays when they spill over. She folds laundry like a pro—especially those fitted sheets— and Mom's a skilled cook. No SpaghettiOs for her family, only homemade sauces, roasts with perfectly browned and tender vegetables, and delicious moist cornbread. She doesn't mind my culinary curiosity, my intrusions at her elbow. I pull up a stool and bump her arm as I study her techniques for red velvet cake: the exact measurements of sugar and flour, baking soda, baking powder, cocoa, eggs, vanilla, and a pinch of salt. I beg for a taste of the Crisco. "Sarah, I know it looks like frosting, but it's shortening; it has no flavor at all." I still beg, until she gives me a small spoon with enough to convince me I never want to taste it again.

She takes pride in the intellect God gave her. Some days I come home from school at 3:00 and find her curled up with a book that Rosemary or Molly recommended. She works as a substitute teacher for the public schools, sporadically, earning $29 a day. Every month or so, it seems, some teacher at McKinley Vocational is called for jury duty, scheduled for surgery, or off on maternity leave.

After a two- or three-day stint, she's back home testing her knowledge on *Jeopardy!* or laughing out loud at the comedians on *Hollywood Squares.* She has perfect penmanship, too, even when she fills in the tiny squares of a newspaper crossword puzzle. Sometimes, I hear her eliciting Dad's help. "You know what a callipygian is, Honey?" He might go straight to his dictionary. "Aha! 'Having well-shaped buttocks.'" Dad keeps his super-thick copy of *Funk & Wagnalls* on a tall, wooden stand in a corner of the dining room. At its base is a hideous, carved wooden gargoyle the size of a pet dog; Dad considers it a true work of art. I hate that thing. On a Christmas Eve, after Dad had already had a few drinks, my older siblings gifted him with said dictionary. When he unwrapped the gift, his orneriness took him straight to the *F* pages to make sure it contained his favorite four-letter word. The only time I hear Dad utter the word is when he's out-of-his-mind drunk.

For the rest of the evening, we hear about callipygian Mom. After numerous highballs, Mom's hips loosen up, and she waggles down the hall to the kitchen to make them both another drink. Indeed, we've settled into our 1920s, three-story home. The size of our new home is double the size of the home we left. Our parents' drinking has doubled too.

IT'S SATURDAY, and by the time the Saturday morning cartoons are over, the Sara Lee jingle "Nobody does it like Sara Lee" is stuck in my head. But I change the words to "Nobody doesn't like Sarah Lou." The packaged cakes aren't all that popular with us. We prefer fresh, glazed doughnuts.

As I toss away the remnants of two strawberry Pop-Tarts, the dry crusts hit bottom where Mom has just placed a fresh trash-can liner.

I swallow the last of my milk. The front doorbell rings. It's my new friend Jessica.

"Please don't call me Jessica," she says. "I hate that name. Call me Jess." She's come to escort me over to her neighborhood. Though we both live in Woodsdale, I've never crossed Bethany Pike or seen Jess's house. She wants to show me the shortcut.

The highway traffic can be heavy. We're careful. We pause next to the guardrail and look left, then right. We wait for a city bus to chug past, fart its fumes, and move along. Jess and I hold our noses, cough, and laugh. Behind the bus is a posse of ponytailed motorcyclists in sleeveless T-shirts and red bandanas. Easy riders. They pass us one by one. The last biker is followed closely by a topless Corvette convertible headed up to Oglebay Park, no doubt. The driver, in aviator sunglasses, waves to us. Jess and I wave back. We smile at each other. We're in shorts and tank tops, which are way better than the uniforms we're stuck with Monday through Friday.

Jess stands with one leg forward ready to dart. I bolt when she does. We sprint across the double-yellow line to the opposite guardrail, which Jess clears in a leap. I follow suit. She runs at a good clip down her neighbor's backyard. She doesn't look back. I follow the leader, doing the quickstep, down a path that's been worn flat by lots of short-cutters. We mount the rise of a sprawling estate with a manicured lawn. Miniature shrubs outline a side entrance of a three-story, brick mansion, creating a semicircular courtyard. A slate paver path leads to a private, fenced-in tennis court. When do the owners have time to play? People with this much house must work a lot of over-time.

As we clear the first property, another beauty comes into view: an enormous cottage in gray stone and brown cedar shakes, with a slate roof, and fenced in by ten-foot-tall, crew-cut shrubs. We tread up the edge of the property.

"Wow." I gawk like a Beverly Hills tourist. Even the arched, wooden front door looks like something out of a fairy tale. "Once upon a time," I say, and Jess laughs. But I seriously wonder what else we might see on this field trip. How do the owners feel about our trespassing?

"The red-brick belongs to the Williamses," Jess says. "My older sister stays there and keeps an eye on things when they're out of town. They pay her. This one's the Howards' house. They don't care if we cut through."

Jess lives in a big house on Hamilton Avenue, next to these on Hawthorne Court. Her house is a mansion too; but, she has eleven brothers and sisters, so it doesn't feel quite as spacious as it might otherwise.

ON JUNE 21ST, I wake up to lots of activity downstairs. Mom and Dad are celebrating their twenty-fifth wedding anniversary with an open house. I've never heard of a silver anniversary, but Molly and Robby arrived the night before to help Mom arrange for this afternoon's gathering. Molly sets out a shiny new sterling silver tea set, a gift to our parents from their adult children. Mom is thrilled with the roomy silver tray that holds a large coffee pitcher, creamer, and sugar bowl. She displays the gift on the new buffet she purchased along with new dining room furniture.

Dad and Mom's best friends are Matthew and Stella Green. Matthew's manager of the Ashland, Kentucky, plant, and he's worked with Dad on previous projects. Stella and Matthew have no children. Mom and Dad claim that Matthew doesn't like kids, but they don't seem to mind us. They become regulars at our house. I'm told that as a wee toddler, I forced myself up onto Matthew's lap so he was forced to hold me. Everybody got a big kick out of Matthew's grin, his heart melting as he held a baby in his lap who looks just like Bunzy.

Usually, Dad and Matthew go to Dad's basement workshop so Dad can show off his newest clock or tool invention or tell dirty jokes. Mom and Stella sit in the living room chatting and laughing. After an hour or so, the adults reconvene in the living room to shuffle the cards. The adults laugh louder. Matthew slurs his words, including his favorite cuss word toward his wife. She comes right back at him. She uses the *f-bomb*. I'm convinced Matthew and Stella hate each other. But by morning, all is forgiven.

Matthew and Stella Green are back and spend the night. Stella's diabetic and gives herself a shot of insulin every morning. She has a simple routine, and she calls us kids to the kitchen to watch.

"Hurry up, John," I say. "Stella's about to pull down her pants!" Hannah, John, and I hover around her backside, eager to see her fleshy butt.

"Give me some room, kids," she says.

She extracts a long needle, holding it up in the air like Dr. Geoffrey. She pulls a tiny vial of liquid out of her makeup kit and fills the needle. She wears elastic-waist pants. She pulls down the side to reveal her naked butt cheek. In seconds, it's over. Now, she'll break off the sharp end and give us the empty syringe that we use to give each other shots when we play doctor. The insulin allows Stella to drink a certain number of highballs.

LATER THAT SUMMER, Hannah, John, and I are dropped off for a week at our Granny's farm in Green Bank. One evening after the sun has descended behind the mountains and it's so dark I can't see my hand in front of my face, I follow John into Granny's sewing room off the kitchen.

"Salou, come here, I've got to tell you something," John whispers. This is what he calls me now: Salou. He has combined my first and middle names, Sarah and Louise, and this pet name sticks.

There's a pass-through window between Granny's sewing room and her bedroom. John turns on the little lamp, perches himself up on the sill, then, slides onto Granny's bed. He lies down on his stomach facing me. I sit across from him on the other side of that window, waiting. I can tell whatever he has to report is going to be very private.

"I know what comes out of a man's penis," he says. "Not when they're peeing but other times." My eyes must've been as big as saucers. "You want to know?" he asks.

"Gosh, no, John. What are you talking about?"

"It's true. I've seen it. It's kinda yellow, and it squirts out."

I make a face and turn away. I'm not sure I believe him. Plus, this is not how our week at Granny's is supposed to go. Whenever we've stayed at the farm before, it's been a Tom Sawyer and Becky kind of adventure for us: John and I catching minnows down on Deer Creek; playing with the crawdads that hide under loose, muddy rocks; imitating the cows that moo at us from the adjacent farm; and talking about how we're going to convince Granny to let us take another ride on Farmer Brown's tractor. John is ruining it. My stomach hurts.

When we return home, I keep my distance from John for a few days, but he sulks around and eventually I let him back in my good graces. We watch silly cartoons and laugh. I don't tell anybody in our family what he's described. I don't want to tattle this time. But as the weeks pass by, he seeks me out to talk about sex. Whether we're in my bedroom or his, he nags me to playact some sex act. Repulsed, I leave the room. I may be curious but not *that* curious.

With our new home, our new school, and our new friends, there's plenty clamoring for our attention. Couldn't he just stop already? That day back at Granny's, I'd acquired some ancient knowledge that I was not supposed to have and, at seven years old, was way too sophisticated to accept. Men's penises were none of my business, and I was glad I didn't have one. But a few months later, when John and I are upstairs, John begs me to play like we're adults. He bribes me with the offer of a quarter.

"C'mon," he pleads. "I promise. I swear I'll never ask you to do it again." Though we've been taking baths together since I could sit up, we rarely see each other naked now. And since that time at Granny's,

I surmised that maybe John had performed some act on the teenage pervert who had abused him in Virginia. But I didn't say so. The idea disgusted me and so did the thought of penises.

John misinterprets my hesitancy as possibility. He gets a hopeful look on his face. "No, John, no way. I just couldn't—I wouldn't—do that." But he won't give up. Being with John is like being with my other self. I can read his face. We can be ourselves; we can say anything to each other. Sometimes, we finish each other's sentences.

I close the bedroom door. He says he'll pay me a quarter.

"I already told you no, and I meant it." Though I've drawn the line, I figure, if I just go along with some aspect of his fantasy, it will satisfy him, and then he'll leave me alone. I figure I can convince him, "Whatever we do stays strictly between us." Maybe I want to make up for all the times my tattling got him in trouble. Maybe I can make up for whatever's been taken from him. I decide no money will be necessary, but I'm calling the shots. He can lie on top of me for two seconds. That's it. "And don't tell a soul."

Nothing happens. But somehow Mom gets the idea we've "done it." When I hear her tell my older siblings, I deny it, red-faced, and flee the room.

Two Different Worlds

"WHERE DO THE NUNS PUT THEIR BABIES?" I ask over and over again. Hannah, John, and I have begun Catholic school. Our homeroom nuns at St. Mike's grade school wear floor-length, long-sleeved, black gowns and black headdresses that include long black veils. Their flesh, what you can see of it, is smooth; their white hands, spotless. On their left-hand third finger is a wedding band. I assume they're married. They wear silver crosses hung on a long strand around their necks. They wear no makeup, never pluck an eyebrow, and seldom ever smile. When I discover that the nuns live together across the street from our school, I'm baffled. Is that where they put their babies?

We've been called to the kitchen where Dad joins Mom in telling us the facts of life. Dad has tears in his eyes. "Sex is the greatest thing ever between a man and woman," Dad says with a catch in his throat. *If it's so darn good, then why are you crying*, I think.

"Sarah, nuns don't have babies. I've already told you: they don't get married. Those are religious rings they're wearing. To have a baby takes a man and a woman." Mom's answer doesn't satisfy me. "But where does Sister Mary Teresa put her babies?"

At the end of the session, we're admonished not to run out and tell our friends. I go immediately to my friend Cindy's house and tell her everything.

OUR FIRST FEW YEARS at St. Mike's are real eye-openers. The church building next to our school takes up an entire block. Somewhere on the parish property is a massive statue of Saint Michael the Archangel sporting intricately carved wings, slightly outspread and taller than the saint himself. Two evil serpents are coiled in tame submission at his feet. He is my first superhero since Big Chief. I imagine St. Mike scaling tall buildings. His eyes scan the neighborhood for sinners, and occasionally, he looks directly at me. By third grade, though, the place gives me a guilty conscience.

Sundays are holy days of obligation when Catholics are expected to attend mass; also, each Friday we kids go to mass with nuns and our lay teachers sitting directly behind us. We follow the rules. Lines of children enter the nave of the church in silence, stopping just inside the door to dip our fingertips into the holy water in the deep, carved marble bowl and make the sign of the cross touching the forehead, then heart, and both shoulders. We proceed up the aisle in single file, genuflect, and enter a pew quietly, sideways, facing the altar. Lower the kneeler. Kneel. Fold hands. Bow head. Pray. Await further instruction.

If we deviate from the rules, a nun who has zero tolerance for irreverence will box our ears or smack us upside the head with the palm of her hand. John, and most of the boys in my class, will feel her firm hand after mass or in the school hallway when they whisper or step out of line. I do fine in church until John jokes, "he who farts in church sits in his own pew." A giggle escapes my lips.

The church often holds the heavy scent of incense that's emitted from the lantern-like censer that hangs from a chain and is swung back and forth during certain rituals and holy days. At these times, the priest steps down from the altar dressed in floor-length, pale satin garments and processes down the center aisle swinging the censer toward parishioners. When I get a good whiff, it makes my nose tingle and my face flush. I envision prayers floating to heaven and evil spirits exiting the building. Church incense triggers Mom's cough and her urge to smoke a Camel.

The organ plays softly from the second-story choir loft. Mass begins. I gawk at the art in this virtual museum. A life-sized St. Joseph stands pensive. Jesus and Mary stand near the altar rail. The twelve Apostles and other Biblical figures are rendered in stained glass on dozens of tall windows. Massive marble columns, more solid than oak trees, hold up the church ceiling. Brass pendant lights hung high overhead and suspended from long, brass chains draw my gaze upward.

Up front, on either side of the altar rail, tiers of votive candles flicker in front of a small table. One person at a time can occupy the short, padded kneeler in front of the candles. We're encouraged to stop by after mass, light a candle, and offer up a prayer of intention. Each flame represents a prayer. A nearby coin box invites donations that ensure the candle supply. I wonder if adding money with your prayers increases the likelihood of their being answered. Along the side aisle hang the fourteen Stations of the Cross, each one six feet apart from the next. During Lent, students walk the aisle in procession, pausing at each of the Stations.

JOHN SERVES AS AN ALTAR BOY at Sunday mass. I watch for him to enter the altar area. With his red, full-length altar garb over his clothes, he looks like a little priest. He carries a long, brass candlelighter that reaches the tips of two high, beeswax candles. Heavy brass chalices hold the Communion bread and wine and are covered with stiff, square linen palls. A large, brass book stand holds a missal whose pages display the prayers of the mass for the priest. The book's long, red ribbon helps the priest hold his place in these prayers.

At the consecration of the bread and wine, John and his fellow altar boy kneel on either side of the priest, appearing to me like Old Testament angels on the sides of the Ark of the Covenant. At the instant the priest raises the bread and then the wine, in consecration, I hear the sound of bells softly ringing. This signifies the elements are now Jesus's body and blood. I'm supposed to keep my eyes shut, but I peek. The brass bells are at John's knees, and I fear he might not pick them up in time. But he pays close attention. He barely looks at the sacred bells as he lifts them. His eyes are on the chalice. The bells ring. The miracle is performed. Maybe John will become a priest. Not if Dad has anything to say about it.

The central figure above the altar is a life-sized, crucified Christ on a cross, arms outstretched and head hung low. Heavy nails plunge deep into blood-stained hands and feet; a wicked crown of thorns pierces the bloodied forehead. The sight of our Savior on the cross makes me anxious.

When I'm in third grade, I make my First Holy Communion. First, though, I must make my first confession in one of the heavily draped confessional booths off the side aisles of the church nave, the sight of which fills me with dread.

It's Saturday afternoon. A soft-shoed priest opens the center door of the triple-doored confessional and waits patiently for penitents to enter and to kneel before an opaque screen that hides penitent from priest. I must enter one of those places, and the man with direct access to God will listen to me recount my sins. I fear I've committed more sins than all of the priests combined have heard. Where would I begin?

But my first confession goes smoothly. I tell the priest I neglected my prayers and missed church on Sunday, sins that Mom suggested. My sins don't faze the priest. He gives me prayers to recite as penance: an Our Father, a Hail Mary, and a Glory Be. I must be no worse than the forty other third-graders lined up in the aisle.

For my class's First Holy Communion, I wear a white dress and a lace veil, and matching white socks and shoes. I look like a miniature bride. I fold my hands, walk in procession, kneel at the altar rail, close my eyes, and stick out my tongue. I've been told to let the bread melt on your tongue—don't ever touch the Host; and to chew it would be disrespectful.

IN THE MID-SIXTIES, Wheeling's population is close to 50,000. The traffic as we walk to and from school and church presents danger. One dark and rainy morning, I walk down to the bus stop in my rain boots and stand alone in front of the public school where the Catholic-school bus will pick me up and take me to St. Mike's. The traffic on Route 88 is heavy. My umbrella keeps me dry as I watch and wait. Commuters, their lights on, their windshield wipers flashing back and forth, their wet tires hissing on the pavement, pass swiftly by. When traffic slows, drivers honk their horns. I wonder why my bus is late.

A beige hatchback with a thin, brown accent stripe across the door slows in front of me. I stare at the male driver. Why did he stop? He reaches over to roll down the passenger window. He smiles. I draw closer, figuring he needs directions or something. His pants are unzipped, and he is fondling himself. I back up, turn my face away, and freeze. I want to run, but I'm gripped with fear. I ignore him. He takes off. But out of the corner of my eye, I see him make a right turn at the next block. As soon as I know his car is behind the large, public school building where he can't see me, I run to the school's big front entry. I hide behind one of the wide, cement columns. I peek out and see the car again, slowing to where I'd been standing moments before. The driver inches his way forward, then makes the right turn again. Finally, my bus arrives. I run down the steps, race for the bus's open door, and climb aboard. I collapse onto a seat bench, my heart beating so fast it is making me sick. My stomach is in such knots by the time I arrive at St. Mike's, I am ill. An elderly priest walking by me in the hallway, takes one look and asks, "Dear, what's wrong? Should you go call your mother?" I nod, whimpering. He accompanies me to the principal's office.

"Mom," I cry on the phone, "come get me now. I'm sick!" She comes right away and takes me home. She follows me upstairs to my room and sits on my bedside. "Sarah, what's wrong?"

"I just don't feel good."

"Okay, lie here and rest." But before she can leave, I grab her arm. "Mom, some man followed me today." I tell her about him slowing down, and how I figured he needed directions. I tell her how he came around the block again and again.

"He didn't expose himself to you, did he?" The word "expose" shakes me to my core. At the split second she asks, I know that's what he'd done. "Oh, no, Momma," I say, as if I'm being accused of something and need to cover up for the pervert's actions. For months, even years after, when I walk the streets of Woodsdale—home from school, to my friend's house, or down the street to babysit for a neighbor—I look for that ugly hatchback car with the creepy man. I mentally rehearse what I will do if I see it: run up to the nearest neighbor's porch. I often expect to see it coming around the bend. But I never do.

MOSTLY, THOUGH, LIFE ON OUR STREET is predictable and sweet. By day, our parents are approachable, even kind. Mom helps me with homework; I can share news about school or get her signature on a paper I need to turn in. But after a certain hour, after a few highballs, her handwriting becomes illegible.

We dodge Dad. It's easy. He's a man of routine. He comes home from work, fixes a drink, and stays in the living room until he has a late supper in the kitchen and goes to bed. It especially makes sense for John to avoid Dad. The verbal abuse has escalated. Dad's alcohol-fueled nerve escalates, increasing the buildup to whatever frenzy is brewing, like a smokestack ready to blow. He stands up from the corner of the sofa, pulls his shoulders back, clears his throat, and spreads his feet for balance lest he toddle and lose all credibility. When Dad gets red-faced and angry, John is always to blame.

"I said, get in here!" Dad yells. Here comes John, tears already forming in the corners of his eyes, like he's walking to his own hanging. He wipes the tears away before Dad can see them; but once he faces the monster, his head and eyes are low. This goes on for years, and John develops the look of an awkward, overweight, passive boy. At times, Hannah and I side with Mom in trying to get John to study harder and comply with Dad's rules. We both become frustrated when John can't or won't change. Just do what Dad says, please! Stand up straight when you walk past him. Make better grades! And stop crying for heaven's sake!

If John had to worry about bullies at school—and they were there—they held nothing in comparison with Dad. It would have been so nice to hear Dad say to John, "I know you're trying. I'm on your side." "I like the way you talked to your sister just now. That was really kind." "You're doing a good job on that assignment." "I'm proud of you because you're really trying." "I'm sorry." "I forgive you." "I love you."

JOHN GETS RAVE REVIEWS for his morning paper route. At the grocery store someone will ask Mom, "Aren't you John Blizzard's mother?" She pauses, not sure if she should acknowledge the truth just yet. "Why, what has he done?" she usually says.

"That boy of yours is the nicest little fellow when he comes to collect for our newspaper. Always so polite." Mom brings the news home to Dad who's shocked.

John holds his head up a little higher. He trains me to take over his route the summer he visits our sister Molly in Virginia. I get up at the crack of dawn for my training, but that's OK—I'm gonna get paid. I haven't been up at 4:30 since that time at Girl Scout camp when I didn't go to bed until then. The sky is still dark except for a stray star here and there. Streetlights help me see the sidewalk in front of our porch and the thick, fresh bundle of *Wheeling News-Register*s tied up in string. My stomach growls, and I rub my eyes. I'm already planning some toasted, blueberry Pop-Tarts with melted butter on them the minute we get back from the paper route. The air is cool. John and I are dressed in sweat shirts and jeans. I'm barefoot. "Go back in and get some shoes on!" I run upstairs for my flip-flops.

John demonstrates his technique for loading ad circulars, bundling each newspaper, and affixing a tight rubber band. There must be fifty newspapers filling his tan canvas sack. I try not to complain when the newsprint turns my hands gray. I'll scrub them before I eat the Pop-Tarts. He looks especially professional with the wide shoulder strap across his chest. As we walk under the streetlights, he explains his routine and tells me it's important to know the customers' idiosyncrasies: "Never just throw the paper wildly onto their porch. If it lands in the shrubs, go fetch it. Set it up there yourself, you dig?" I follow him to the end of our block. "See Mr. Smith's house? Don't collect from him till he's had his supper. Wait till Sunday night to make your rounds, say, around seven o'clock."

I take mental notes. "Where do I put the money?" He shows me his zippered money bag, tucked down inside his canvas bag. "If they write you a check, give it to Mom. She'll cash it for me."

"How much am I gettin' paid?" I ask, following him across the street. "Same as me, twelve bucks a week. Plus tips. Don't do anything wrong, or you'll see a big drop in tips." I wonder what he ever did wrong on his route, but I don't ask. I'm tired and he's walking fast. I have to keep up.

"You see Mr. Jones's house, 57 Walnut, the one with the wooden door? Don't hit his front door with the paper, or he might yell at you. Just throw it underhanded like this." John demonstrates.

"Why do I have to be so careful?"

"'Cause Mr. Jones doesn't like the noise. Don't screw up."

John leaves for Virginia and I take over the route. I deliver papers every morning for a week. I develop a knack for the toss. I get a little overconfident. One morning I'm lollygagging along. I take Mr. Jones's newspaper out of the canvas sack, rear back, and toss it overhand with all my might. Then I remember John's warning! I cringe. There's going to be a loud thwack. But Mr. Jones's front door is wide open. The newspaper goes flying down his hallway. I giggle and hurry on with the rest of the route. I can't wait to tell John about my aim.

These are the stories we laugh about. John and I spend the rest of the summer watching cartoons and comedies on Saturday mornings, once he returns from his paper route. We watch *The Three Stooges*: Curly is always making funny faces while being smacked across the face by Moe. Or Curly is dancing with a heavy-set woman who gets fleas up her back. She wiggles uncontrollably like she's doing the Watusi. There's a cartoon with Foghorn Leghorn, a sarcastic rooster with a repertoire of one-liners: "Smart boy, I say smart boy, got a mind like a steel trap. Full of mice." Our favorite cartoon character is Droopy, a dog with a droopy face. We laugh so hard our sides hurt and its lines becomes our punch lines when we want to make each other laugh.

We recall the strange rituals we established in Virginia, like the very important thing we had for Tootsie Pop wrappers. The drawings on the wrappers depict children riding a tricycle, on a skateboard, rolling downhill in a soap-box-derby race car, and other fun activities. I collect the ones that feature a little boy in full Indian headdress shooting a bow and arrow. Reminds me of Big Chief.

WINTER MONTHS IN WEST VIRGINIA are my absolute favorite. Maybe because my birthday falls one month after Christmas. Hannah, John, and I wait with bated breath for the morning's weather report, hoping for a "snow day" that closes the school. If yes, we change from pajamas into snow gear faster than a NASCAR pit crew can change a tire. "Let's see who all's going sled-riding!" Our favorite hill is at Oglebay Park.

The city park in winter surrounds her visitors with a white forest, a wonderland of mature junipers and pines that dwarf us and our sleds.

Clusters of evergreens glisten with snow, and sometimes their branches are coated with shiny ice. Someone brings a four-man toboggan and we fit as many snow-suited rear ends on that huge sled as possible. It's a long, steep, thrilling ride downhill as the fresh snow powder splashes our faces and blinds us to where we're headed. But we land safely. The sensation of speed and adrenaline is worth every step of the laborious climb back up.

Besides my birthday, there are other fun winter rituals. On the very first day we see a substantial amount of snow, Mom makes a big pot of her famous celebration chili that she concocts from finely diced fresh onion and green peppers sautéed in oil; freshly ground chuck; and cans of red kidney beans and tomatoes. A dash of salt, pepper, and sugar, plus heaping tablespoons full of chili powder, paprika, and parsley. Just knowing that comforting goodness is simmering on the stove makes us happy. If roads are clear, and school's in session, I'm the most popular student when I bring a thermos-full to school for lunch. Sometimes, there's enough left over for me to cart the thermos to my friends on sled-riding days. On the school bus, my friends make me smile with their banter. "We know what Sarah Blizzard's having for supper," someone says. "Chili!" reply my fellow passengers. "And with a name like Blizzard, we have her to thank for all the snow days!"

For Dad, winter might not be so much fun. To ensure his car will start in the sub-zero temperatures that West Virginia winters deliver and that he'll make his forty-minute commute to the Cardinal Power Plant in Brilliant, Ohio, Dad props his hood each night and hooks a high-wattage lightbulb to the underside. The heat generated by that bulb prevents the engine from freezing.

ON A SATURDAY AFTERNOON in mid-March, I pull on my jeans, turtleneck, and windbreaker; I finish my glazed doughnut I've hidden on a shelf in the back of the pantry; and I head out and cross the Pike back over to Jess's house. Though the snow has melted and gusty winds remain in the forecast, we're going door-to-door selling Girl Scout cookies. Peanut butter and thin, minty ones are so popular, I expect to sell dozens of boxes and earn a badge. Armed with my order form in its over-sized envelope, I discover Jess has already garnered several orders from her mom and immediate neighbors. We walk off her front porch ready with our sales pitches. We'll take turns doing the talking.

Everyone buys. The envelope bulges with dollar bills. I'm not sure my envelope will hold all the cash from the houses we have yet to approach. Jess assures me some people will write checks. When we turn off of her street and walk quickly round the bend, we see nestled against the emerald hillside the most incredible house in Woodsdale: a four-story, brick mansion that looks like a watercolor painting come to life. There's no gate or fence, but it appears too exclusive to approach.

"How in the heck do you get in?" The long driveway leads to a massive set of front steps.

"I'm not going up there," Jess says. "That place gives me the creeps."

"I'll do all the talking," I volunteer. This is practically a neighbor of hers. What's she afraid of? She stands firm, shaking her head. "You go," she says.

"Okay," I say, "but you wait right here for me."

I climb the long driveway and dozens of steps to a massive mahogany front door. I press the button of the decorative brass doorbell. No answer. I try again. Still no answer. I turn to see if Jess is still in sight. I can just make out the top of her dark, shiny head of hair right where I left her. I'm about to abandon all hope of selling any cookies at this house when the front door opens.

A hefty, gray-haired black lady wearing a well-worn apron looks down at me. "What do you want?" she says. Her tone says she has more important things to do than listen to my sales pitch. "Would you like to buy some Girl Scout cookies?" I ask in my sweetest voice.

"Come on in," she says, opening wide the massive door. I stand stiffly in the foyer, trying not to gawk at the crystal chandelier hanging twenty feet overhead. As she closes the door, I notice a brown feather duster in her thick hand. The place smells like Pledge. "The Missus might want to order some," she says. "Over there, push the button, go to the second floor. She's upstairs." She disappears.

I walk across a sleek, tile floor to the first residential elevator I've ever seen. I take a deep breath and press the button. The doors open up right away. I step in and find the only button on the wall. I press it, and the paneled doors close up. I'm in a veritable closet and it's rising. After a few seconds, the cage stops abruptly and the doors open. I step out gingerly, pull the folder tight to my chest, and pull my shoulders back. I peer around but don't see a soul. I walk down a wide, high-ceilinged, wood-plank hallway lined with tapestry wallpaper. I pass a window whose drapes match the wallpaper. At the arched doorway of a bedroom, I see an old woman sitting in a wheelchair like an invalid I've seen in movies. She has short, gray hair and pale skin. A crocheted afghan covers her knees.

"Who is it?" she asks, squinting. I smile awkwardly, walk right up to her wheelchair that's positioned next to a four-poster bed. "My name is Sarah Blizzard. Would you like to buy some Girl Scout cookies?" I'm not sure she can hear me. I reach in my envelope and hand her my cookie folder, glad to have a focal point other than this complete stranger and her bedroom.

"Where did you say you lived?" she asks.

"Just across Bethany Pike, Ma'am." I gesture out the window. She looks at me and shrugs, then she looks at my order form, opens up the folder, and turns the pages.

"I guess I should buy some," she says. "Put me down for eight boxes."

"Yes, Ma'am! Thank you! Would you like Peanut Butter? Thin Mint? Trefoil?" I point to the pictures.

"I like shortbread," she says. Her voice is weak. "Just mix them up." She reaches down, lifts her pocketbook from its place by her wheelchair, and draws out a checkbook. I tell her the dollar amount. I've added it up.

"You're my best customer today," I say. She slowly enters the figures and scribbles her signature on the bottom, tears out the check, and hands it to me.

"Thank you, again." I smile as I write in her information.

"Will you be delivering them?" she asks.

"Oh, yes Ma'am. In a few weeks."

"Just so you know, I won't be alive when you come." I stare at her, stunned. My face flushes. I step backward. I almost blurt out, *You can't die! Who'll eat all the cookies?*

"Yes, Ma'am," I manage. I turn to leave.

The hall feels stuffy. A wave of regret sweeps over me as I exit her room. What was I thinking coming here all by myself? I look left and right, but I don't see the elevator. I quicken my pace, turn into another hallway; I fear I've gone the wrong way again when a landing and massive, spiral staircase open before me. I grip the handrail and lean against the rounded wall all the way down. Each of my steps lands flat on the widest part of each tread. When I spy the front door, I take the last few steps toward freedom like Cinderella at midnight. Oh, Lord, please don't let her die before I escape! I try to turn the door handle, but it won't budge no matter how hard I tug. My knees are knocking. I want out of here. I need to tell Jess about this place and the old lady.

The housekeeper comes to my rescue. I move aside. She unlocks the door and nonchalantly flips a bolt. As it clicks open, she pauses. "Did she order anything?" she asks, her hand on the door. "Yes, Ma'am," I say, trying not to sound out of breath. "Eight boxes." She opens the door wide and I'm out; I quickstep across the front porch and down the steps to the driveway. I don't stop when I reach Jess. I keep moving and motion for her to follow. "You won't believe what happened to me in there!" I never see the old woman again, but I deliver eight boxes of cookies to the house.

MY CONFIDENCE AS A SALESPERSON builds when I receive a beautiful folder in the mail with Christmas card samples glued to the thick pamphlet. They sparkle with glitter. I can sell them! I'll earn more money than John does for his paper route. I hit the streets. The snowy scenes and religious Madonna and Child cards will sell themselves, I reason. The card company gives me direct profit depending on how many boxes of cards I sell.

The lady directly across the street, Miss Vayhee, opens her door just enough to stick her head out. She's nearly six feet tall and her hair is a wild mass of blondish red curls. I stand up on tiptoes to peek over her shoulder. Why does she act so mysterious? When any of us knock on her door to sell whatever the school is pushing for a fund raiser, she always politely declines. That never stops me from asking. I'm intrigued by her insistence on her privacy, though she always opens the door. Why does she answer it? The rumor is that she had an unplanned pregnancy years before, she had never married, and lives alone since her only son is in the armed services. Years later, I learn she's a hoarder. Maybe it's best she doesn't invite me in.

Another neighbor, Mrs. Dreyfus, is in her eighties and also lives alone. Her favorite pastime is standing out on her front porch loudly cussing at my friend Cindy's little barking Chihuahua across the street. Mrs. Dreyfus's voice scares people away, but that little dog is fearless. Mom befriends the crotchety old woman and asks me to help her on Saturdays. Mrs. Dreyfus pays me five dollars to sweep her kitchen floor and front porch, pull up the sheets on her bed, and empty the used coffee grounds in the garbage. I also collect all the other garbage in the house and carry it outdoors. Too bad we could never get Mrs. Dreyfus to take a short walk one block south, where she might have been able to holler some sense into Miss Vayhee.

The further up the street I go, the nicer the houses become with their wider front porches, stone work, and embellishments—like the black, wrought iron *A* that hangs on the side of Mr. Alexander's exterior, stone fireplace wall. Mr. Alexander, who is also in his eighties, becomes a favorite of John's and mine; he even comes to see me in a play at school after I go to his house and sell him a ticket.

"Come right in!" he says, smiling and gesturing his welcome. Trim and short, with white hair, he holds himself with good posture and looks and talks in a very distinguished manner. He takes time to get to know us, and I recall sitting in his living room telling him all about myself. I make a special trip to his house if I'm selling something. Mr. Alexander is one of John's best newspaper customers too. When he sees her, he always tells Mom how fine her children are.

Another favorite neighbor is Mr. Paul. When the weather's good, he's up on a tall ladder at either his house or his immediate neighbor's—a Mr. Fix It in the flesh. He attends our church and smiles when he sees us at mass. One sunny day when I walk by his house, his ladder is propped up against the red brick, but Mr. Paul is nowhere in sight. I slow down as I walk by, wondering if he's gone indoors for a minute. That's when I see him up on top of the roof, straddling a third-story eave. He looks down and calls out, "Say a Hail Mary for me."

Interacting with the neighbors is a great rehearsal for life. I learn how to talk to older people respectfully, and I realize not every household is like mine. John has customers' approval on his newspaper route, but that's where a healthy interaction with adults ends for him. His main role models are teachers and nuns who never give him a break. His grades are barely passing. From time to time, at school and at home, Mom tries to defend him but John can't seem to thrive.

My favorite person on the planet is my third-grade teacher, Mrs. Kathryn Oliver. She's one of only a few lay teachers at St. Mike's. She's Catholic and has taught for many years. Her hair is practically white, but she has young eyes and a sweet laugh. She seems generally happy, maybe because she knows where her glasses are at all times: they hang from a silver chain she keeps around her neck, over her sensible blouse. She wears knee-length skirts like Mom's.

I talk too much, pester the boys about who they like, pass notes, and chuckle at the jokes we tell when we're supposed to be reading our boring books. But I complete my assignments, and I want to please the teacher. I try to hide the fact that my parents are drunk every weekend, and I try not to let on how gross they can be when they're making out in the living room. The nuns hover, as though they can foretell our wrongdoing. I carry a shame that I'm afraid shows, and I feel a need for confession. But my shame is warranted. Should Mrs. Oliver call in the evening to speak to my parents, she would hear them slur their words. I answer the phone in the evenings. I would say my parents are sick.

Mrs. Oliver points out when I do something well or score high on a test. She's smart. She doesn't play favorites. I look forward to Friday afternoons when she reads aloud from The Boxcar Children, a series of books where amazing children create a home for themselves in an abandoned boxcar in a forest. I love their independence and sense of adventure.

When Mrs. Oliver introduces limericks in our English unit, I'm excited since I'm already familiar with their rhyme meter. Dad has always liked to quote them. Some I could never repeat to Mrs. Oliver, but I catch on quickly to the writing. Then she announces a contest for the third-graders, sponsored by the fourth-graders with whom we share our classroom. The prize for the winning limerick is a large, boxed, white chocolate bunny rabbit with a big pink ribbon around its neck. I don't even like white chocolate. I consider it to be a fake flavor.

But the bunny is so beautiful, with pink sugar eyes and the bow. I want that prize.

That night, I walk into my parents' sacred card-playing space and tell them about my contest. "Do you guys have any ideas for what kind of limerick I should write?"

"Why don't you write about someone from Wheeling?" Mom says. That's all the inspiration I need.

> *"There was an old lady from Wheeling.*
> *While playing cards, she loved dealing.*
> *If you didn't let her deal,*
> *how loud she would squeal!*
> *That's why the lady from Wheeling is dealing."*

MRS. OLIVER CHALLENGES US TO PRAY some very special prayers during the Holy Week that leads to Easter Sunday. "Students, Easter is this coming Sunday. Who can tell the class what happened on Good Friday?"

Several students raise their hands. Jesus died on Good Friday. "That's right," she says. "And based on Scripture, we believe His death was at three in the afternoon. Keep this in mind, because I'm giving you a very special homework assignment." We take out our planners and prepare to write.

"You'll be on Easter break on Good Friday. No matter where you are, I want you to go somewhere by yourself at three o'clock, maybe to your bedroom. Find a quiet place. Close the door. Get down on your knees and say a prayer. Make three requests or wishes to God. Within the next year, at least one of your requests will come to pass."

I do as Mrs. Oliver asks. At 3:00 p.m. on Good Friday, I run up the stairs to my room and close the door. I get down on my knees next to my bed, bow my head, and pray. I make three requests, one that I'll never forget: God, you know Mrs. Oliver, my third-grade teacher? Next year, I'm likely to end up in Mrs. Klug's or Mrs. Klettner's class. My last wish is for you to make Mrs. Oliver my teacher again."

The next fall, Mrs. Oliver is promoted exclusively to fourth grade, and I am assigned to her class. Ever since, no matter where I am at three on Good Friday, I make three prayer requests.

One afternoon in fourth grade, Mrs. Oliver says, "Students, take out your pencil and a sheet of paper. You're going to hand this in, but don't write your names on it." With the overhead projector, she displays a photograph of a dark, rain-soaked street; small puddles fill potholes; the water glistens in the streetlights. Shadowy figures lurk along the borders. "Write about how the picture makes you feel." The room gets quiet. "Write the first thing that comes into your mind."

I write, "This picture puts me in a dark and dreary mood. I feel like I want to curl up inside a closet all alone and hide from the world." Mrs. Oliver looks through what we've handed in and reads mine aloud. I blush and keep very quiet so nobody knows it's mine. But I think she knows.

BY NOW, Mom trusts John and me to walk the three miles to church for mass. The Saturday 5:00 p.m. folk mass is like a new show in town. At this lively liturgy, guitars and upbeat songs replace the traditional hymns. We leave home in plenty of time to enjoy ourselves along the way. We wave to neighbors who watch us from their deep front porches. We walk practically in step through his paper route. He recalls some of his favorite customers: "Mr. Alexander always gives the best tips. He gave me a whole dollar last week, not a quarter or two like everybody else." We pass from the sidewalks of our street to Walnut to Poplar and then Maple and over to Heiskell Avenue before we reach "the path," a trail secluded by tall, dense hedges and mature trees that hide centuries-old mansions on either side. At least one of the homes—where I'll babysit later on—has an elevator. The house is huge. I'm sure the elevator must lead to a haunted turret, so I stay in the kitchen and family room and make the kids tuck themselves in.

Once through the path, we're mere blocks from the church. We stop by the Minute Market for penny candy bought with coins intended for the collection plate. Ella works the cash register. She's too thin in her oversized housedress, and her stringy, gray hair looks like she's taken dull scissors to it. Even when we're her only customers, Ella seems nervous and anxious to ring up our purchases.

If we have thirty-five cents left, we sometimes stop at Colonel's soda shop for a slushy Wizzard. Just past the market and soda shop are a bowling alley and a barbershop. I always check my appearance in the reflection on the picture windows we pass.

JOHN'S CLASS AND MINE COMBINE to prepare to become Soldiers for Christ in the Sacrament of Confirmation. I'm excited to select my confirmation name. All my friends select Theresa, which baffles me. Don't they want to choose their own name? I choose Christine. It sounds pretty and sophisticated. We line up to get approval for our new name from Sister Margaret Mary. She looks expectant, like she's secretly hoping someone will choose Margaret. She's pleased with my selection, the feminine form of Christ. Maybe I'll become a nun. Not if Dad has anything to say about it.

The Saturday afternoon before confirmation, my neighborhood friend Teresa and I are riding our bikes up the street. We stop at the noise of several boys playing in their crude clubhouse. They spy us coming and duck inside, but we can still hear their laughter behind the thin walls. I dump my bike in the yard and find a milk crate to stand on. I peer through a crack in the siding to see what's so damn funny. One of them pulls down his pants.

I jump back, grab my bike, and move to the sidewalk, motioning for Teresa to follow me. I whisper what the boy has done. "Eww." She blushes and looks extremely uncomfortable. Teresa is never mean or unkind, much less dirty-minded or inappropriate. I feel holy just being around her. Her entire family is religious; one of her older brothers is studying for the priesthood. The mention of a naked boy makes me feel I've corrupted her. Teresa looks at her wristwatch.

"It's time for confession. I gotta go," she says, releasing her kickstand.

"Maybe I should come too." With confirmation just days away, I feel the need to get right with God after seeing a boy who's not in my family naked. What will I say to the priest? Maybe I'll just hint at what happened. He'll figure it out and help me, like a doctor handing out a prescription.

We ride in silence. I'm worried. This won't be my standard confession about neglecting prayers, lying, and missing mass. I have seen a boy's naked body, but also I told Cindy, the day before her birthday party, what gift Lisa was getting her. I'm a horrible person! If I'm to remain friends with a good person like Teresa, I must provide the priest with enough information to absolve me of my sins.

Teresa and I kneel quietly in the pew. I watch out of the corner of my eye for my opportunity to enter the confessional. Teresa seems anxious to get hers over with. I'm in no hurry. The sanctuary is silent. I can hear whispers of a person making their confession. It's a solemn ritual, and Teresa and I don't say one word to each other. We don't ask who should go first. She looks at me when it's time, and I nod for her to go. After a minute inside, my friend pulls back the heavy, red drape and exits the confessional. She's finished already.

My insides are churning and my palms are sweaty. I get up and walk slowly into the confessional, pull the curtain closed, and sit down, ramrod straight on the tiny wooden chair. A priest's aged hand slowly slides back the dark panel, revealing a mesh screen and his shadowy silhouette. Kind of like the window between Granny's bedroom and sewing room, where John confessed his own secrets to me. But here the priest and I are not face-to-face. He keeps his gaze away. I try not to look at his profile. I make the sign of the cross and whisper, "Bless me Father, for I have sinned. My last confession was a month ago. I've lied and not kept holy the Sabbath. And I've, I've committed adultery."

"What do you mean by adultery?"

"I saw a boy pull down his pants. He was naked," I whisper.

"Say three Hail Marys, two Our Fathers, and one Glory Be," he says.

"Thank you, Father." I am relieved beyond words. You never need to tell the priest all your sins, just the worst ones. On the ride home, I feel so free I barely touch the handlebars.

The bishop of Wheeling himself officiates at our confirmation service. He looks exceptionally powerful in his tall, stiff miter, which resembles a cone-shaped crown. His long, silk robe is embroidered with Christian symbols—a lamb looks lovingly up toward Jesus, the shepherd. The stole around the bishop's neck is embroidered in gold thread. We're forewarned not to stare when he enters the church, but we find ways to gawk at the eight-foot-tall spectacle with its brass shepherd's crook.

Altar boys follow his every move. When it's time for the bishop to call my class forward, my palms sweat. I breathe in short spurts. I have an urgent need to pee but fear that if I leave my pew I'll miss my confirmation. I won't become a Soldier for Christ. I won't be Christine. So I pee right there in the pew. I hope no one notices that I'm sitting in a wet spot; but my sister-in-law, Ed's wife, who is sitting behind me, leans forward and discovers what has happened. She practically pushes me away from the student sitting next to me. The ceremony continues. I act like nothing has happened.

The Summer of Mom

IN SUMMERS, we attend Oglebay Park's Day Camp, where I learn to swim. Swimming is my greatest summer joy—floating, diving from the side. My form matters to me. It's exhilarating plunging into the deepest part of the pool, head first and toes pointed, to emerge from the side and squeeze out my long, wet ponytail. I embrace summer's heat on my shoulders, a warm smile of sunshine from God. I develop a more athletic body. I don't play organized sports, but I push myself to swim, bike, and run.

One unforgettable summer, Dad announces he will have to stay at work for maybe two months. When he says the plant strike forces him to remain at work for an unforeseen amount of time, probably weeks, we try to understand, but we wonder how Mom will cope. We watch her for any signs of fretting; she seems resigned to the idea. She doesn't grumble or whine or ask "How long?" So maybe it's a good thing? Even Dad seems okay with it.

Eventually, we accept that since our dad is management, he has no choice but to stay inside the plant during the strike for his own safety. He considers the union's demands unreasonable, and he's going to live up to his reputation as a loyal company worker. He will not come home. He will not cross the picket line. He warns Mom, "Negotiations aren't going well between management and the union. The union guys will be armed with rifles and dangerous, if anyone so much as sneezes near their picket line. If I want to keep the power plant running, I'll have to stay inside. If I can arrange it, I'll sneak out occasionally, but then I'll have to sneak back in during the night. It could be weeks, months."

We also couldn't anticipate that Mom wouldn't drink a drop of alcohol while Dad was away, and John, who relaxes now that Dad's away, seems much happier.

Every other weekend or so, Mom sneaks out for a ritual visit with Dad. She follows his orders: "Drive to a set of railroad tracks near the Ohio River, and wait with the headlights and the engine off. Be there at exactly 12:15 a.m. I'll find you." They rendezvous, speed back to Wheeling for a few hours together, then Mom delivers Dad back to the meeting place before sunup the next morning.

Having a Mom 24/7 is like nothing we've ever experienced. She cooks lots of tasty vegetables. She loses ten pounds. She takes us to Elby's and lets us order Slim Jims, onion rings, and hot fudge ice-cream cake. She takes us to the drive-in movie to see *Fools' Parade*, featuring Jimmy Stewart, George Kennedy, Kurt Russell, and Anne Baxter, and shot at the West Virginia State Prison in Moundsville, nearby in Marshall County.

During filming, my friend Jess and I are at an open window above the sidewalk where Mr. Stewart is walking with an umbrella. Jess's dad is editor of the *News-Register*. He knows people and gets us onto the set. We can see the production lights positioned along the streets. "Hi, Mr. Stewart," I yell. He looks up at us hanging out the window and waves his umbrella. I can't wait for Mom to see that part of the movie.

When she takes us to Wheeling Park pool, I have Mom all to myself for the first time since I was five and all my siblings were in school. In the past, she just dropped us off for a few hours. I was used to being there alone or with Hannah and John. I stare at swimmers lined up on the rungs of the fifteen-foot ladder ready to show off with swan dives, jackknives, and cannonballs. I usually find a friend in the sunning area and place my towel and swim bag next to theirs. "Anybody need Coppertone?" The wide, warm sidewalks glisten with water dumped by cannonballs.

It's a thrill to have Mom's undivided attention, yet strange to have her there. I revert to age five, insisting she "Watch me!" as I do handstands, hold my breath underwater, and swim the breaststroke from one side of the pool to the other until I'm so waterlogged Mom suggests I "lay out" a spell. With her watching and encouraging me—"That was wonderful, Sarah!"—I feel alive, significant, and valued. She tells me she'd been a swimmer herself and could've tried out for the Olympics. I believe her. Mom is never one to put on airs. I wonder what else I don't know about her. I ask her more questions those weeks than I ever have in my life.

ONE NIGHT, well into the strike, when Hannah, John, and I are outside playing with the kids from the neighborhood, Mom yells, "Time to come in!" The streetlights aren't even on yet.

"Why do we have to come in so early?"

"We're taking a drive. Get in the car."

She has a new station wagon that she drives down Route 88 and on to National Road.

"I want to drive by those union guys. See their picket line for myself." She drives to Brilliant, Ohio, past the factories along the Ohio River, then slowly past the smokestacks of Dad's hydroelectric power plant. We arrive just before sunset. There it is: the picket line. The men, rifles at the ready, have set up a blockade with their card tables. Ten restless union members stand around watching the traffic.

"I'm going to drive past and then turn around," Mom says. "On our return, I want you to roll down your windows and stick out your tongues at them." We do as we're told. Then, we roll up the windows, curl up in the back seat, and hold our stomachs as we laugh ourselves silly. Those idyllic weeks are soon over, and Mom and Dad pick up where they left off.

Dad earns a lot of overtime pay during that strike. That fall, he and Mom fly to Italy with Matthew and Stella. Ed babysits, and when Mom and Dad return, they tell us about the Sistine Chapel, the Trevi Fountain, the statue of David, and all about the grandfather clock Dad repaired in the lobby of their Italian hotel.

I'M ELEVEN THAT YEAR when Ed leaves for Washington, DC, and a new job. It's late summer, and when he's gone, I rearrange his bedroom. I pull the twin bed away from the wall and reposition it next to the screened window. I realize I can lie here at night. The room I share with Hannah on the other side of the house can be unbearably hot and stuffy. This room has two doors and a window. With all three open, the room catches a cross-breeze. This will be my haven.

Lying back on the pillow, despite sleepiness, I recite the words to my memorized Catholic prayers. "Come Holy Spirit, fill the hearts of the faithful, and kindle in them the fire of your love." Prayer comforts me at bedtime like nothing else. I've known the Lord's Prayer by heart since I was three or four. I might start on my knees, then hop up on my mattress and sense the loving arms of God wrapped around me. One such night, I lie in the dark facing the open window with the pillow scrunched up under my neck. My prayer attention wanes as I get sleepy. Background sounds of highway traffic, my dad's clocks ticking, and a random dog barking barely register. A light breeze cools my face. My gaze is drawn to the neighborhood scene. My eyes float over four back-yards softly lit by a distant streetlight, the next-door neighbor's back sidewalk, Mrs. Radcliff's clothesline, the Hudsons' doghouse. In the fur-thest distance, about three hundred yards away, directly underneath and highlighted by the streetlamp, I can make out Cindy's enormous tree. We've played kick-the-can with the tree trunk as our base. "Olly, Olly, in—come free!" Whoever's "it" calls in those still hiding when our game is over. The streetlamp's timer triggers an end to our play and sets off Mom's alarm: if we don't head home upon illumination, Mom comes to the back stoop and yells, "Kids, time to come in!"

As my eyes become fixed on the scene, a remarkable sight catches my attention. I sit up straight in bed. But when I do, the phenomenon disappears. It's only from a reclining position that I can see it. I lie back down, my eyes peeled for the spectacle. It's so miraculous, I don't dare blink, lest it disappear like vapor or a dream upon waking. But I'm not asleep. With my nose up close to the screen, I blink hard, expecting to break the spell. But there it is again: Jesus's profile, perfectly outlined by the branches on Cindy's tree. As if God Himself has sketched the Savior's face in silhouette with a glow-pen—his forehead, nose, and bearded chin tilting up toward heaven. It's as if Christ Himself is saying, "Child, I hear your prayers."

My faith increases one hundredfold. I don't tell a soul, but I go to that window nightly, searching for the Savior's visage and filled with peace when I find it again and again.

Many Catholics travel far distances to witness manifestations of Jesus's or Mary's presence. In one case, witnesses claimed tears could be seen falling from the eyes of a statue of the Virgin Mother. I imagine inviting pilgrims to my house: "You have to go up into my brother's bedroom at night after the streetlight comes on. Lie down in his bed, just so, with your head turned toward the screen." People will come from all parts of the world to see what I see; the line will flow down our front stairs, out the door, and down the sidewalk. But I keep it to myself.

By week's end, the manifestation of Christ's profile ceases to have such definitive lines. But during the nights I witness it, I believe the miracle at the window is a reflection of His love.

MOST SCHOOL DAYS, I'm carefree with my classmates. I laugh at myself and chime in when others laugh at me and at each other. But puberty hits me like a Mack Truck. I develop breasts overnight. They're sore.

Anxious moments sweep over me and cause me great distress, which I believe I hide pretty well. I become more sensitive and emotional. I don't like it, but I don't let on. I play the class clown. I lead the comedic charge against substitute teachers. I make fun of them behind their backs, imitate them, and snicker when I should be reading social studies. If someone teases me about my thick thighs or upturned nose, I shoot another joke right back. Still, It doesn't take much for me to feel mortified.

When Mrs. Oliver falls ill and I discover that Mom has accepted the substitute teacher job, I freeze. This is certain disaster. Mom will embarrass me. I go to bed very worried that night. I rehearse potential scenarios. I anticipate the badgering from my peers. What if they can still smell alcohol on Mom's breath? What if she acts prissy or swings her hips when she walks? What if she raises her voice? What if she reprimands one of the boys I have a crush on? To my knowledge, my friends' parents don't drink excessively. At none of the many Friday night slumber parties have I ever seen any parents overindulge. And I've never once invited anyone to spend the night at my house. Too risky. I call Jess for moral support. "It'll be fine," she says. "Man, am I ever glad it's not my mom." "Yeah, well, I wish mine would just stay home."

Mom starts the day asking everyone to "please hand in your homework assignment." My classmates shuffle papers, looking for the work the clueless substitute is referring to. A couple hand in their work, but the rest of us are incredulous. Mom assumes we have it in for her. She lectures us, starting with me.

"Sarah, don't you have your homework?" she says, hands on her hips. I shake my head, my face crimson. "Sarah is setting a fine example, isn't she?" All the boys turn to laugh at me. I want to hide under my desk, run from the room. Mom hasn't bothered to ask *why* some of us don't have our homework. Mrs. Oliver told us the day before that if we memorized the assignment, we wouldn't have to hand anything in.

A fellow student explains. Mom backs off. Never again does she substitute for my class.

WHEN I BEGIN FIFTH GRADE, I've almost reached my full height and development. I'm self-conscious. I can't hide my need for a bra. I'd always laughed along when we made fun of one another in class or on the playground, as if to say, "Go ahead. I can take it. What's *your* problem?" But by November, the words sting.

One afternoon we're sitting at our desks reading aloud from our social studies book. One of the boys reads about milking Mrs. O'Leary's cow. I hear giggling behind me. When I glance back, another boy gestures to his friend about my chest. I'm the cow. I turn bright red. I want to disappear. It takes everything in my power not to cry. The next day, I tell Mom I'm sick and stay home.

When I return, I make matters worse. I assume my friends will laugh uproariously at a clever prank I plan to pull on our teacher, Mrs. Klug. One of the boys had given me a trick ring with a tiny bulb reservoir for water, which you hide in your hand. He demonstrates at our desks before the bell rings for class. "You walk up to someone with your hand in a fist, knuckles up, close to their face, and say, 'Do you like my ring?' When the person admires, the ring, you squirt." I love it. Mrs. Klug, our teacher, will love it too. She's in a good mood this morning. Everyone will laugh.

After she makes the announcements, I walk up to her desk. I hold my fist up to her face, knuckles up, and say, "Mrs. Klug, do you like my ring?" When she looks down to admire it, I squeeze the bulb. Water sprays down rather than up. Now, there's water all over the lapel of her new suit jacket. She asks me in a loud voice, "Do you want the dry-cleaning bill?" My face turns flame red, and I walk back to my desk defeated. My prank has backfired. I want to cry.

PUBERTY USHERS IN ANXIETY. I'm terribly uncomfortable about anything sexual, including my own development. The advancement my body makes toward womanhood—the growth under my armpits and elsewhere—is too much to bear. I'm plagued with fears. And I wonder if my friends ever knew my parents were always drunk.

Most days, I put on a good act, laughing at whatever the guys say, and listening then affirming whatever the girls say. I become someone the boys confide in. "Ask Laura if she likes me," Donnie whispers across the aisle. I dutifully consult her to see if the cheerleader wants to "like" the football player. "She says she'll think about it," I say, giving him a thumbs-up. But if Donnie or Tom or Paul, or Laura or Janie or Mollie, find out what goes on at my house, they'll surely reject me.

My first period comes that month. It is the worst curse imaginable. I cry for three solid days. Mom assumes my older sisters have informed me about everything. They haven't. Not only has no one explained menstruation, but I completely ignore those persistent stains on my panties. I think my hygiene is off. I change them. When Mom does the laundry and confronts me, she tries to be reassuring. "Men have it so much worse," she says. "They have to shave every day."

This is not comforting. I am mortified. How can I tell my skinny, flat-chested friends about this? They already bully me about my development. Now this! And the boys! I've never felt so miserable and stinky and gross and petrified over what it means to be a woman!

I hear Mom tell Dad what her baby is going through. He comes into the den where I'm curled up in a ball on the love seat weeping. I sense his presence. He sits next to me, puts his big strong arm around me, and squeezes my shoulder. His breath is Old Mr. Boston, though he's only on his first glass.

"You're gonna be such a wonderful woman, a wonderful wife and mother someday, just like your mom." I stiffen and turn away sobbing. I want him to leave me alone! He goes back to the adult world that I want nothing to do with.

Though his attention is unwelcome, through the years I recall it as a very tender moment. He tried. But Dad is the last person I want to chat feminine-anything with. He's way too comfortable with sexual talk, and I never understand his obsession. I'm never sure if he worships sex or just sex with Mom. I accept him as a dirty old man whose knowledge of passionate devotion often crosses the line. He tells lurid, adult sex jokes as though he's an immature teenager who enjoys their shock value. I never try to stop him. It would be disrespectful. But I never get used to it.

. . . I smell strong fumes on my parents' breath each evening and imagine their drinks taste a bit stronger than the thick cough syrup from which I've begun to take swigs before heading out to meet my friends. It's prescription strength, and it sits behind the aspirin and laxative in the powder room medicine cabinet. Drinking it warms me clear through.

But the real stuff, the hard liquor in half-gallon jugs, takes up half the kitchen counter space on one end, alongside various shot glasses that never get rinsed out. Bottles never actually empty; they are simply replaced with sealed jugs every Friday when Mom makes her ritual run to the liquor store. Under the counter, in a cabinet, they store half-empty bottles of various brands of vodka, Scotch, and other elixirs they're saving for guests. Hidden and unchecked, they're like orphans waiting for a home . . .

III

Downhill Ride

EVEN AFTER DECADES OF MARRIAGE, the sound of the garage door lifting is Mom's signal to greet Dad by the kitchen door with a kiss and a drink. Friday is especially sweet because Mom's hair, after a week with no washing, has been transformed at the beauty shop into a teased and sprayed shiny silver helmet. Dad squeezes her buttocks.

He runs down the events of his day. With fly ash settled like eyeliner beneath his eyes, I can just picture him—the power plant maintenance supervisor, working around every kind of power plant residue. Mom listens attentively. When she gets up to pour them another drink, Dad gets up, too, to check a clock's tick. Mom returns, drinks in hand, for their card game.

When the drinks take effect, though, Dad loses his temper with us. He gives Mom deep kisses in front of us and growls with a passion I don't need to witness. He talks about the satisfaction of his sex life. He waxes on about the beauty of love. He thinks priests, men who devote their lives to God, are hypocrites. But when we leave for church on Sunday, he still says, "Don't forget to pray for me." Mom converted to Catholicism in her mid-thirties, and our parents send all six of us to parochial schools. It's confusing to follow the Catholic discipline of weekly mass, recitation of the rosary, the Stations of the Cross, confession, mass attendance on holy days and then to return to a universe without rules when our parents drink. The sacraments, the commandments, and all the rest fly out the proverbial window.

Despite their daily drinking at home, Mom and Dad hold it together during the week. Dad's job at the power plant sounds exhausting. He seems to be physically and mentally tired from supervising the crew. Even with his complaints and aggravations, Dad has a strong work ethic. He never misses work, even when he's hungover. Before five, sometimes 6:30 p.m., Mom and Dad are honest, available, funny, and hardworking—like solid citizens. We learn to play canasta, which is nothing like bridge. The object of the game is to collect sets of the same card and score the most points. We know every aspect of the game—two-, three-, or four-handed play. With four hands, I'm always Dad's partner. John is Mom's. We play for an hour or two, until one of us reaches 5000 points.

I sit tight-lipped, studying my hand across the table from Dad. Never would I hint what I hold in my hand. But when it's my turn, and the card I've been waiting for shows up on the discard pile, I whoop and holler like I've won a prize. John will do the same. Mom and Dad are more measured. When John and I oppose each other, it's us against them, a winner-take-all mentality, and John is my Enemy Number One. Mom and Dad are experts, but they seem to enjoy playing us.

One night we have a marathon round. Both our teams have melded, scored enough points on the board. One of us freezes the pile by placing a wild card as the discard. That means the only person who can pick up the discard pile is one who has a natural pair. The pile grows and grows. Nobody can pick it up.

The tension grows thick between John and me. It's like we're playing cutthroat poker for high stakes. The clocks ticking adds to the suspense. Whoever draws the right card will get to pick up the entire pile filled with canastas and all those points. The pile is so high now, it threatens to fall. Someone is bound to draw the necessary card soon. I take deep breaths, convinced that pile will soon be mine. This goes on for ten minutes until I discard a card that brings a gleam to John's eye.

He lays down the cards needed to pick up the pile and takes it.

I scoot away from the card table. I then jump up out of the chair, turn my back on the play, and run up the stairs to my room, crying like a baby.

DAD'S CLOCK HOBBY takes all of his spare time. He can repair any size clock, any style, though he prefers antiques. He'll make house calls for folks who have no clue how to maintain clocks that they've purchased at a furniture store or an antique market. He has clocks from neighbors, maybe a brass mantel clock or an anniversary clock. He's smart with mechanical things, adept with his clock tools, and he has an engineer's mind when he's sober. He develops an ear for the sound a pendulum is supposed to make when a clock is in perfect balance.

He acquires some very high-quality timepieces. Some are valuable on the market and to collectors. Our counter tops, mantels, and the perimeter floor space are full wall-to-wall with clocks. Grandfathers, pendulum clocks, anniversary clocks, and even ship clocks, which have a unique balancing mechanism. Turn them upside down, and they'll still keep good time, even when fastened to the wall of a great ship on the high seas during a storm.

Dad also collects a variety of melodic cuckoo clocks. Most of them wind up with a key. Some are weight-driven. Many of them chime at the quarter, half, and top of the hour. They are his pets. I am so used to their sound in the background that I don't hear them tick or chime.

A Seth Thomas banjo clock, so rare it's hard to put a price on, hangs in the living room. Eli Terry, Ansonia, Waterbury, and New Haven Clock Company clocks all reside in our home. But one timepiece, a tall grandfather clock in a cherrywood case, the Andrew Dunlop clock, stately and beautiful, is the most valuable of all. Dad is surprised to discover how rare it is: the builder made clocks between 1701 and 1732. Dad's is in mint condition.

I revere Dad's taste in clocks and the way he loses himself inside the case of a clock, intent on its maintenance. All the dinging makes him happy and gives him something to do on Sunday while we're in church. Those Sundays before he retires, Dad rarely has a drink before late afternoon. His hands are steady as he takes apart a complex clock. When we return from mass, he's still hovering over his card table with magnifying glasses on his head. Every brass hand and coil spring is clean and oiled. He sets the oven on low, lays out gears and other clock pieces on racks to air-dry, then rebuilds the mechanism meticulously as though it's a complicated jigsaw puzzle. Sometimes, I think he is a genius.

GENERATION TO GENERATION, families feel the effects of ancestral strongholds. And hand-me-downs can include a whole lot more than just heirlooms.

My sisters Rosemary and Molly both live in Virginia, and each hosts our entire family from time to time. Molly is the more maternal. But from early on, even before I arrive at my teen years, it's Rosemary I want to emulate. I adore Abingdon's charm. I'm the only one of the six born in her town, and the only one born in Virginia.

Rosemary's antebellum mansion on East Valley Street is saved from demolition when she and Geoffrey rescue the dilapidating Litchfield Hall, which was built in the 1830s. Following months of rehabilitation, their restored home becomes my standard for cool sophistication: informal, large, bohemian, and comfortable. It remains one of many fine restored residences on the neighborhood's tree-lined streets.

When I enter its wooden front door and stand in the grand foyer, I feel embraced by a welcoming friend. I love the expansive wood floors and plaster walls that soar thirty feet above my head and are capped by cove crown-molding so old it can't be reproduced. I will never love a house more than I love this one. The grand space feels regal, yet mysterious. The rooms are sparsely furnished, almost minimalist.

My brother-in-law's desk fills a corner of the twenty-by-twelve living room. His law books fill the built-in bookcases on either side of a fireplace that's topped by a carved, wood mantel. An antique armoire in solid mahogany that Rosemary and Geoffrey acquired on one of their trips to Europe stands guard on the far wall that is otherwise unoccupied.

In the adjacent library, a rust-colored, corduroy, L-shaped sectional rests along two walls. A single, pillared candle, wax puddles gracefully alongside, rests on the wood-burning fireplace's mantel. It says to me, "I light here every evening."

After everyone has gone to bed on the second floor, I lie awake listening for ghosts. They must be friendly since the place feels so special to me. But when I hear creaks on the wooden staircase, I pull my covers tightly under my chin. If this mansion in the heart of Appalachia does harbor ghosts, they're likely phantoms of runaway slaves or soldiers in the battle for freedom who are storied to have found shelter in Litchfield Hall's basement during the Civil War.

Just past the foyer and down the hallway to the left is the formal dining hall whose focal point is exquisite French cut-glass doors, which look like something out of *Architectural Digest*. The doors flank a glass and wrought iron dining table where ten guests can linger for a leisurely lunch of Rosemary's beef Burgundy, homemade rolls, salad with a tasty dressing, and French silk pie. Everyone enjoys Rosemary's deep-throated laughter, which—along with the clever conversation—is as much a part of the meal as the cuisine.

The French doors, I conclude, explain why my sister and brother-in-law bought the house. They needed no restoration. They are jaw-dropping, yet tasteful, spectacles; conversation starters as ornate as palace gates shipped from Versailles. To be in that ethereal space and witness what happens every afternoon, weather permitting, makes me feel extremely privileged. As the sun travels over the western, private

courtyard beyond the beveled-glass doors, sunbeams come searching for entry to this grand space. Light meanders through the mature
oaks, through the beveled-glass panes, and onto the dining room walls.
Guests say, "Cheers!" and splash toasts of Guinness to the light show
driven by the prism effect of the glass as the beams hit the curved glass
just so, and the light changes direction. It becomes liberated, dancing
in miniature rainbows up and down the plaster walls. Colorful, flickering butterflies alight, performing on my sister's fortunate canvas. I
adore the spectacle in this lovely, historic home.

Rosemary and Geoffrey enjoy a rich social life in Abingdon. Her
friends stop by often. Some stay for the gourmet meal she prepares.
One or two card players are always available for hands of bridge with
Rosemary and our parents. Or, there's the front porch, with its high
beadboard ceiling, where one can catch a gentle breeze in the hot summer. The porch swing is a splendid spot unless Rosemary's contrary cat
curls up on the seat cushion, hissing at family and visitors.

OFTEN, I'M ALL JOHN HAS; but just as often, I'm not enough. If John
skips a barbershop appointment and his hair grows past his shoulders,
Dad lashes out at his appearance. If John needs both parents' signatures on something because he's gotten poor grades, he's summoned to
the living room. He slouches into the room, his feet heavy as if he wore
steel-toe boots. We all hear the language Dad uses on John, language
usually reserved for the strongest offenders. But John has never been
tough, and Dad doesn't seem to care. Dad cusses and demeans John for
as long as it takes to break him. "You're no good!" "You're nothing but a
thug!" "You're going to end up in prison!"

Though I'd never invite a friend to spend the night at our house,
I hope for invites to spend the night with friends. School is a refuge
where I put aside the familial stress for six hours, more when I have a
Brownie or, when I'm older, a Girl Scout—Cadette—meeting. My bond

with Jess, who has eleven siblings, means I spend numerous nights at her house. We curl up under a big blanket on her sofa and watch movies. Sometimes we sneak into the formal living room where her older sister keeps her albums. We play Janis Ian's "At Seventeen." The lyrics are too advanced for us, but we both like to pretend we're older.

It's a rainy day. My neighborhood buddy Teresa and I can't ride bikes so, even though I seldom invite anyone to the house, I invite her. I take her to the basement where we listen to the radio's Top 40 and we're inspired. "Let's write our own song!" I say. I grab one of Mom's pads of paper from the kitchen counter. Teresa helps me when I get stuck. I can still remember the words to "I Don't Feel Real."

Sunshine . . . rain . . . I just don't feel the same. I just feel the way you shouldn't feel, and all I can say is: I don't feel real. You make me feel the way I do. I can't see your real reason too. Did I do something to make you this way? I don't know but all I can say is: I don't feel real. The way I feel, the way I feel, I just don't feel real. I just wish that maybe someday I'll feel real.

I'm excited. Teresa acts enthused, and we plan to share our talent at the radio station. The disc jockey announces the radio station phone number regularly. He urges listeners to call in with requests. Hannah usually requests the song that makes her stop everything and sing about her current crush: "Cherish is the word I use to describe all the feeling that I have hiding here for you inside . . ."

The DJ answers. Teresa and I are both nervous, but Teresa is also shy so I do the talking. This could be our big break! In a rush, breathless for the opportunity to be on air, I announce in my eager young writer voice that we've written a masterpiece. "We'll sing it for you!" I don't give him a chance to respond. We sing a line, and he thanks us for calling.

I HAVE GOOD TIMES WITH ED, and I like being treated like I'm grown up. He takes us to see *Hush . . . Hush, Sweet Charlotte* on the outdoor, drive-in movie screen down the road from our granny's, in Green Bank, West Virginia. I've become desensitized. I don't react as I did at a Vincent Price film when I was little. Now, I fixate on the acting of legends like Bette Davis, Olivia de Havilland, and Agnes Moorehead. The film becomes one of my all-time favorite Hollywood classics.

Ed's drop-dead-gorgeous best friend, Jack Lerner, makes me feel flush all over when he's at our house. When Jack comes over to cut our grass one day, Mom asks me, "Would you like to take Jack some fresh lemonade?" I sit with a pitcher of the cool drink on our back stoop, posing for Jack by crossing my legs—like my mom does—every time he and his lawn mower are facing my way.

When Ed dates and later marries his first wife, I duck for cover. Hannah, John, and I will never measure up to her standards. When we eat, she criticizes the way we smack our lips or fail to use a napkin. She asks Hannah and me to be junior bridesmaids in the wedding. But when she realizes we've failed to bring slips to our shopping expedition for trying on dresses, her pained expression tells us she sees us as country bumpkins.

But Hannah and I can't avoid the surprise wedding shower her bridesmaids have for her in West Liberty. At the banquet hall where the shower takes place, I meander around the expansive food table. Everyone forgets I'm there. While my sister-in-law-to-be opens gifts, ladies come over to the food table and fill their plates. I stand next to a platter of what must be at least fifty delicious-looking, tiny, triangular, chicken salad sandwiches. When the ladies have all gone back to their seats, I eat until I practically empty the platter, then I move away so no one will suspect I've made a complete pig of myself. When we get home, I'm as sick as a dog. I never do that again.

The wedding's the first weekend in August. During the pre-wedding festivities at the house, on an evening when all of our adult siblings and their spouses are present, I stand at the top of the stairs, leaning over the banister to spy on the crowd gathered in the living room. Every seat is filled. Friends of the family are there too. Adults sit side by side on the sofa. The chairs, ottoman, and even some of the armrests are taken. Dad's voice booms above the rest. He's drunk.

Dad's ability to hold his liquor—we call it his "drinking credibility"—takes another hit one night on our front lawn when Ed invites his new in-laws to our house. Our parents seldom venture out in the evenings; it's rare for them to even sit out on the front porch. This night our drunk patriarch accepts Ed's father-in-law's challenge to a fistfight.

Dad towers over the slightly built man, who's as drunk as Dad. They both take a fighting stance. Dad's a sure bet in a fight, especially with someone half his size. But a fight in our front yard? I'm mortified to think my friends could be driving down our street any minute and might spy my dad getting his head popped off, reminiscent of the classic Rock 'Em Sock 'Em Robots game. The spectacle might have been comical if the two men weren't so pathetic. Fortunately, the brawl lasts just minutes. Whatever fueled the fight quickly sizzles. No one swings a punch. But the incident leaves an indelible mark as to just how unclassy the drinking has become.

I **NOTICE A NEW TENSION** on Geoffrey's face. Rosemary matches our parents drink for drink. On their next visit, any rules left governing our home have taken flight with the already missing, much needed training. When Rosemary arrived earlier that day, she had set her toiletry case on the floor under the pedestal sink in our upstairs bathroom. To John and me, Rosemary's case glows under the bathroom light like a treasure box. John suggests we rummage through it. He digs out a tall can of Aqua Net hairspray. I know this is a bad idea. He removes the cap and sprays the bathroom mirror with the sticky aerosol. I cough as the heavy mist fills the tiny space.

John and I are typical—nice one minute, cruel the next. I decide to make a sharp turn toward cruel. I descend halfway down the front stairs and tattle. Someone's going to get blamed for this so I act as quarterback, throwing the ball of blame into the huddle below. Dad stands up, balances his large frame in a wide stance and turns toward me. He calls John's name once, then a second time, louder. John appears on the step above me, frozen stiff with fear.

"Get down here!" Dad's voice booms. John descends slowly. Dad insists he come into the living room in front of the adults.

"I didn't do anything," John's voice quivers.

My big mouth!

"Don't lie to me!" Dad says. "Tell me the Goddamn truth!" John shakes his head, refusing to fess up. Dad makes a production of taking off his belt, pulling it out of the last loop, and slinging it into the air with a snapping sound. He exaggerates each strike, raising his arm higher each time he hits John. "Lying is the one thing I forbid!" he yells.

I back up and grip the handrail. I'm desperate for this to stop, but it won't. Even if it did, what about tomorrow, next week? My heart races a guilty chant: "You! You caused this!" The belt lashes crack out.

"Stop it, for God's sake!" Mom calls.

Other adults are uncomfortable. Dad's audience turns against him. "Enough!" Dad releases his prey, replaces his belt, and breathes hard from the exertion.

John runs past me, crying. I'm shame-filled and humiliated.

He could've said, "Sarah, would you knock it off already? Stop tellin' Mom and Dad everything we do. I'm gettin' killed here!" Or maybe he did. Maybe part of me believed John deserved the beatings for being so weak, so gullible, so easily led years ago by that boy pervert. But my tattling has become a fierce weapon.

The trauma I witness from the stairs makes me conclude I could be next. Even so, responsibility for my brother's beating is more than I want to carry. For the first time, I see my mouth as a catalyst for physical abuse. I've become a member of Dad's ugly team, a guilty operative in the family abuse network.

After the demeaning incident in the living room, Dad's continuing abuse of John solidly progresses from verbal to physical, though the verbal continues. To extract myself from blame, I listen in as Dad and Mom talk over cards. If I hear of Dad's plans to confront John on the latest infraction, I warn my brother. But avoiding Dad entirely is nearly impossible. If John naively chooses to walk in the front door, it's too late.

Some time after the hairspray affair, from the safety of my bedroom, I hear Dad marching upstairs and across the hall to confront John in his room. I hear a loud smack and Dad retreating. When I check on John, he's crying. "He sucker-punched me," is all he says. I have no idea what that means, but I get the impression Dad has caught John off guard. My brother's okay but furious. We establish a goal: stay as far below Dad's radar as possible.

CALLING 9-1-1 is not an option I'm aware of. I doubt I could have turned Dad in, anyway. It takes me years to process what goes on in our family, especially my own part in it. All I know now is how awful I feel in the smoke-filled, alcohol-fueled, waiting-for-the-shoe-to-drop atmosphere.

I regret that I don't warn John more. It's impossible to adequately comfort him after the worst of the abuse. Our family roles and labels— me the mascot, he the scapegoat—separate us. We descend to survival of the fittest. I dare not move too close to the scapegoat. Home becomes a place of unpredictable behavior, and I'm determined to stay clear of Dad, to guard against any more blame or shame. But if I remain Dad's accomplice in judging my brother's shortcomings, I become an abuser too. The thought of turning on my brother becomes unthinkable. So, I become a sleuth, eavesdropping on conversations. I grow an antenna.

"Where're the kids?" Dad begins.

"Hannah's at Anna's. John hasn't come home from school yet. Sarah's upstairs, I think," Mom says.

"Has John collected from his newspaper customers this week?" Dad asks.

"I don't think so," Mom says.

"Wait till I get ahold of him," Dad gulps his whiskey.

I need to warn John. Dad's reminder to John to collect his payments could escalate into, "You're no good! You're a thug. You're gonna end up in prison!" Dad might summon me next. I take off my mascot Super Girl cape and don the red bullfighter's cape.

I don't tattle on John or anyone else anymore. I withhold information from Mom even when I consider the times she's been a good friend to me and a good listener. Mom and I have special moments when she focuses on me with loving compassion. She sometimes senses when I'm out of sorts or when a headache develops into a migraine. When one comes over me, I'm in so much pain by the time I tell her, I'm crying. I don't know why it's happening. Weeping makes it much worse. I become completely helpless and collapse on my bed. She comes to my room and turns off the overhead light. She sits at the side of the bed and comforts me. She lays a cool, damp washcloth on my forehead, and in a minute turns it to the remaining cool side. She gives me two aspirin. She speaks very softly. "Lie still, Sarah. Don't move, Sweetie. That's what helps your father."

Dad has these too? I can't think straight about anything, but later I wonder if his are the result of hangovers. I will soon suffer tremendous hangovers; but, now, I imagine migraines are hormonal. I feel like I'm being punished for living. I wonder, *What could I have done to deserve this?*

"The first time this happened to your father, we were young, and we were out on a picnic. He didn't have anything with him to take; ever since, he keeps aspirin with him. He won't be without it." I vow to do the same. "You'll be okay in a little while." I was.

AS NURTURING AS SHE IS THAT DAY, Mom and Dad increasingly become hands-off parents. Rosemary, Molly, and Ed recall them being much more involved. Now, our Catholic school education, with its emphasis on discipline and orderliness, is supposed to mold us. Our conduct grade is very important to them. If we earn less than an A in deportment, we're given a verbal reprimand at home.

In school, there are clearly defined rules: Never talk back. Always say, "Yes, Sister; No, Sister." Do your homework. I develop a competitive spirit for spelling bees and comprehension tests. I learn quickly and make excellent grades. Despite the emotions inherent with rapid-fire development into puberty and having become quite two-faced, I do make friends. Joe, one of my favorites, reminds me of John. Joe's always in trouble, especially in the hallway between classes when we're supposed to walk single file. When he turns to joke with those of us closest to him, he steps out of line. The nuns don't think Joe is funny. Sister Seraphina pulls Joe out of line by his ear, twisting it between her bony fingers, and marching him to the wall for a lecture. "Quiet!" Sister spits the last *T* inches from his face. I flinch at the abuse. Though Joe makes me laugh, I try to control my response. I could be next.

I seldom see John at school. I'm detached from the reprimands he endures, but witnessing Joe receiving his gives me an education. I figure John's been enduring such wrath from the nuns on a regular basis. I hope he's able to do as Joe does. Joe brushes it off as soon as he joins me back in line. Joe's my buddy. Our names are only a letter apart so, in line or at our desks, he's usually right behind me. He's my comic relief from the regimented aspects of Catholic school. If the nuns get on my last nerve, there's Joe, mimicking them behind their backs. I hide my giggles. For the most part.

If I do glimpse Hannah and John between classes, at lunchtime, on the playground, or at Friday mass, we give each other silly, wide-eyed expressions. When the nuns look the other way, we stick out our tongues at each other.

We tell Mom how cruel the nuns can be to the boys. Though she never calls the school, she seems sympathetic when John defends himself. When John brings home a bad conduct report, Hannah and I testify to how mean and unreasonable the nuns can be. We cite how other boys are pulled aside and roughed up.

HANNAH AND I know unfairness when we see it, but we can't stop the abuse John faces at home. Dad is a certified rabble-rouser, ready to incite chaos and insist loudly that his opinion is the only one that matters. Watching Dad's unwarranted demands on our brother makes it seem like Dad and the nuns have taken the same lessons. He is utterly and completely disappointed with everything pertaining to John: John's appearance and attitude reflect poorly on the Blizzard name. His hair's too long. Both his conduct and handwriting grades are F. Instead of investigating the hows and whys of John's bad marks, Dad simply finds John unacceptable. And if all of Dad's scrutiny is supposed to spark some improvement in his son, Dad is failing miserably.

The abuse escalates. So often he's told: "Hold your shoulders back!" "Act like a man!" "You're just no good!" "You're nothing but a thug!" and "You're gonna end up in prison!" Hannah and I fear the hammer may fall on us at any second. The three of us forge an even stronger bond. Upstairs in our room with the door closed, we girls can talk. Hannah shares with me what she and her friends are up to, who likes who. We talk for hours about Mom and Dad, our family, and what's going on with everyone. We agree that Mom's and Dad's drinking is unhealthy. We're ashamed of our parents. Our late night sharing from the comfort of our twin beds before we drift off to sleep helps make life sweeter. We may fight over the new sweater in our shared closet, but our tiffs are short and intense, and extinguished as fast as they fire up. We three are a coalition. If we hear John come up the back steps after school, we invite him to our room and listen to James Taylor on the stereo. We like John's long hair, which is way past his ears. We ask about his friends, most of whom are pretty cute. Occasionally, we confer on our parent's gross and drunken behavior the night before. "Did you see how swollen Dad's lip got? Disgusting," I say. Dad's enlarged lower lip is a telltale sign he's completely waxed. And his open flirtations with Mom drive us away.

ONE LONG WEEKEND in the late spring, Mom and Dad drive Hannah, John, and me to the Potomac River side of Virginia where Ed and his wife teach school. When we arrive, we're told about a possible adventure for the very next morning. "I have a student in my class whose parents own an eel fishery," says my sister-in-law. "Since Ed and I both have to work tomorrow, would you all like to go out on their boat for the day?"

"Sure."

"You'll need to be ready early," she says. "You have to be at the boat launch at 5:00 a.m."

Mom, Dad, Hannah, John, and I wake before sunrise, pull on bathing suits, T-shirts and shorts—in case we get to swim—and then load the cooler with sandwiches and fruit. Off we go. At the docks, I can't believe my eyes. This is a bona fide fishing operation. Right on the Potomac River is an expansive manufacturing plant. Adjacent to the plant is a mansion with floor-to-ceiling glass windows overlooking a cove.

We unload our gear. An older man in rubber overalls greets us. A native of Holland, he has a thick accent and wears wooden shoes! "My son and I will be your guides. Come and meet my wife," the man says.

We walk into a vast expanse of kitchen, living room, and dining room, all combined on one large main floor. Several ultramodern furniture groupings separate the spaces, like something out of a magazine. Against one wall are four reading chairs. In the center of the family room, two long, tufted sofas face each other. The dining room area is offset by a large wooden table and matching buffet table with impressive candlestick lamps. I'm speechless.

It's a spectacular day for many reasons, including that our family is getting along. The water is calm and only a few fishermen are out. The bright seagulls take their first flight. The Dutchman and his son tell us how they lay nets for eel. Their manufacturing plant processes the exotic delicacy and exports it overseas. My parents are fascinated.

By the time the Dutchman is ready to board, Hannah is developing a crush on his son. He has dark tanned skin, and his blond hair matches hers. He's about her age.

"Have any of you ever been water-skiing?" he asks.

We haven't. "Once we lay all the nets, we can cruise to an island where I can teach you to ski," he says. The morning is becoming more exciting. Father and son attach a speedboat to the back of the large fishing vessel. Hannah, John, and I count the hours until we reach the mysterious island and try our hands at skiing.

At last, the fishing boat pulls up to the sandbar of an uninhabited island. We're glad we won't have a wide audience when we fall or fail to follow skiing instructions. "Grip the crossbar like this." Our new friend demonstrates from deeper water. "Pull your knees up in this position and keep the rope between them. When I give the boat gas, you'll feel your body thrust forward, but lean back a little and straighten up your legs. If you start to lose your balance, just let go of the rope. I'll pull the boat back around and start over again." He is patient and seems to enjoy our inexperience, and he wants to teach his new friends proper technique.

It takes several tries before I can stay upright on the long, awkward fiberglass skis. I enjoy being pulled in position by the skilled young boater in his little speedboat. We progress well enough to ski up to the island and release the rope right before we reach the sandbar. What a great experience.

Also on the Potomac, Mom and Dad take us to George Washington's Mount Vernon. There, Dad notices that a clock on the mantel in the drawing room isn't running. He inquires why.

"Sir, we haven't been able to keep the thing level, I guess." Dad hands him his clock-repairman's card, introduces himself, and goes on to share his knowledge of the inner workings of antique clocks as well as his experience repairing them. He offers to take the clock back to Ed's home and work on it. The tour guide asks his boss and the next thing we know, Dad is shaking hands with the historic site's acquisitions manager, who gives Dad permission to cart off the antique clock. The staff is impressed with Dad's willingness to spend his vacation tinkering with their timepiece.

Back at Ed's, Dad spreads the valued parts across Ed's breakfast table. In two days' time, he's got the thing doing everything it was built to do: it chimes on the half hour and hour, and it ticks consistently. When he and Mom return the repaired collectible, Dad's reward thrills us all. He refuses to accept any monetary compensation, so the staff pulls fresh vegetables from the garden. My parents return with a garbage bag filled with cabbage, tomatoes, and leaf lettuce.

MOM'S THREE MATERNAL GREAT AUNTS helped raise our mom when their sister, Mom's mother, was widowed and had to go to work. Now, they are all retired school teachers and are coming from Huntington for a visit. They're on their way to Bethany College, thirty miles north up Route 88, for a school reunion and will pass through Wheeling on their way. Bethany has special meaning for our family. Mom says her ancestors, members of Disciples of Christ, the denomination that founded Bethany, donated the land on which the original college was built.

In anticipation of their arrival, Mom cleans the house from top to bottom and puts away the liquor bottles and shot glasses that normally sit out on the counter. While she serves finger sandwiches, potato salad, and chips to the great aunts and their spouses for lunch, everyone's on their best behavior. I'm happy to see extended family. I smile politely. I recall the previous summer when Mom drove Hannah, John, and me to the homestead for a family reunion at a farmhouse with a sprawling yard on land where Mom had been raised. The huge three-story white, wood-framed house sits under an elm that is taller than the house and accommodates the entire family. I feel awkward among family we barely know and that I can't keep straight.

But we're greeted warmly by individuals whose nose, eyes, and cheekbones are just like Mom's, and they seem genuinely pleased that our mom has come and brought her youngest three children with her.

Mom grabs me by the elbow and leads me, John, and Hannah over to some of her cousins. "This is Aunt Dolly's son, and these are his children …" On and on she goes introducing aunts, uncles, and cousins as we try to keep them all straight. One is a famous basketball coach at Auburn, Alabama. We meet him and his brothers. Another smiles or laughs. There's talk of the second cousin who survived the *Titanic* disaster. Among all these relatives, Mom is young again. It's a joyful occasion for her.

I know not to pry about Mom's sister and brother, whom she rarely speaks of and who are absent from the reunion. If I did, Mom would answer with short, curt explanations and get quiet. But these are the people who raised her, encouraged her to read, to make good grades. Maybe they encouraged her to take home economics and those Fanny Farmer–inspired cooking classes.

A line of long folding tables covered with cloths is set up in the shade of the tree whose welcoming branches are outstretched overhead. We gravitate toward the platters of fried chicken and sliced ham, fresh green beans and macaroni salads, and homemade cakes, cookies, and pies that are being spread out before fifty or more cousins, second cousins, and cousins once removed.

As we take our place in line to fill our plates, Mom spies someone she recognizes, but doesn't speak to her. She turns to warn us. "Stay away from her." Was she a lunatic or something? John and I want a closer look at the short, plump lady with a tight gray bun and beady eyes. She's filling her plate ahead of us. Her eyes dart around and seldom make eye contact with others. She looks a bit strange, so we heed Mom's warning. Did the woman do something to our mother back in the day? I don't dare ask. The caution from Mom is all I need, but I sneak a look at her whenever I get bored.

We all stand quietly while someone says a blessing and, after we eat, someone passes around songbooks. One of Mom's aunts leads the singing of "West Virginia Hills," a song I've never heard—even though it's one of our state songs:

"Oh, the West Virginia hills!
How majestic and how grand,
With their summits bathed in glory,
Like our Prince Immanuel's Land!
Is it any wonder then,
That my heart with rapture thrills,
As I stand once more with loved ones
On those West Virginia hills?"

Mom's relatives sing with church choir voices like she does, in perfect tune and harmony. It sounds as if these bright, strong, and intellectual women have written the song themselves.

WHENEVER OUR FAMILY'S MONOTONOUS ROUTINE changes in the slightest, especially when extended family or friends come to visit us,

Hannah, John, and I meet upstairs in one of our bedrooms to rehearse the details.

"Rosemary and Geoffrey will be here tomorrow night," Hannah says, looking out the window for the first signs of snow. The late afternoon clouds are heavy, and the temperatures have dropped below freezing. Rosemary's young daughter and son are like siblings to me. My eyes light up at the thought of Rosemary's visit. She'll be wearing her big, turquoise ring on her lovely, tanned hands.

"Are they back from London?" I ask. Geoffrey has won a lucrative legal case. When he and Rosemary traveled across Europe that fall, they'd rented their own car, which, in my mind, elevated them to the level of celebrity, like Sean Connery and his Bond girls. I can picture Rosemary in the passenger seat while Geoffrey drives on the left-hand side of the road. Now, they're coming for Thanksgiving in Wheeling.

The next morning, the sun is doing what it does most Novembers: peek out at us but refuse to overcome the clouds. Mom and Dad discuss the weather and are relieved to hear the treacherous West Virginia Turnpike south of Charleston is clear. By the time Rosemary and her family walk in the door that afternoon, before Geoffrey can take off his winter jacket, Hannah, John, and I bombard him. On their previous visit, he'd made us a scavenger hunt, and we're eager for another. As our niece and nephew exit the back door to ride the bikes we've outgrown, we seek our brother-in-law's challenging diversion.

"Oh, all right, I guess. Just leave me alone to think about it." We make ourselves scarce. Hannah and I hover over a Monopoly board spread out on the square ottoman in the den. John's the banker. Hannah and I are too excited over the potential scavenger hunt to fight over which game piece to use. My favorite is the thimble, similar to the one Mom uses when she sews. Hannah likes the Scottie dog. John takes the car. We hope we won't be there long enough for an entire game. I pay only half-hearted attention when I land on St. Charles Place.

THE TV is set to another episode of *Andy Griffith* when we hear Geoffrey head out the back door with Ed. We rush into the kitchen. "Where're they going?" we ask Mom who's setting casserole dishes onto the kitchen counter. "They'll be back after a while," she says. Ed is taking Geoffrey for a walk. They're headed to Tom's Bar on Edgington Lane. We're crestfallen. There went our scavenger hunt. When the guys return a few hours later, we figure Geoffrey has forgotten all about it. But he hasn't. "Come here, kids," he shouts from the kitchen. We were so excited it might have been a call from Santa himself.

"Not so fast," he says. "Remember how this works? I've written out all the clues, but you've got to go upstairs. Up in your room, close the door. Stay put till I hide all the clues."

"How many do we have?" John asks.

"Ten. Now go upstairs. I'll call you down when I'm ready to hand you the first one."

We take the stairs two at a time. When we reach the landing, I whisper, "Let's make phone calls." We sneak into Mom and Dad's bedroom. The narrow space next to their bed becomes a magnet for Hannah, John, and me to have private boy–girl phone conversations with friends—when the parents are downstairs, of course. It's also where we make prank calls out of earshot of our parents, who night after night play cards and drink. Mostly, we call Alma Henderson. The legend is that she's working for the Wheeling mob as a madam, running a house of ill repute in one of the run-down apartments on the river bank. We wait for Alma to answer because we know she will eventually pick up. She always answers her phone. We cover our receiver while we giggle. Then we just sit there. No matter how many times she's pranked, Alma answers with a loud "Hello!?" We say nothing. We just wait—until she screams and cusses us out.

Afterward, we gather in Hannah's and my bedroom, and we close the door. I check my Timex wristwatch a dozen times. John reads the collages on my wall, which I made from photos and words in Hannah's old *Seventeen* magazines. "Pretty clothes," he reads and laughs. Underneath the bold type are models in plaid skirts and knee socks. "Ha! Those are so ugly."

"Not as ugly as our school uniforms," Hannah says, turning on her clock radio. Twenty minutes later, Geoffrey calls, "Ready!"

We practically trip over each other getting down the stairs. In the kitchen, Geoffrey's laughing with Rosemary and Mom as they take turns stirring spaghetti sauce. Geoffrey hands Hannah a tightly folded first piece of paper. "When you discover all ten, there'll be a prize for each of you at the end."

Geoffrey walks outside to the back porch; the screen door slams. Hannah unfolds the paper and reads aloud. John and I hold our breath with excitement.

"Inglenook."

"I have never heard that word. What in the world does it mean?"

"Go ask him," John says.

"No, you go ask him."

Geoffrey's watching his kids race down the alley. "We need help on this first clue," I say.

"Go look it up," he says.

We go to Dad's fat *Funk & Wagnalls* dictionary on its stand in the dining room. Hannah finds the word. "Inglenook: an area with a seat at a large, open fireplace. Fireplace!" We speed to the living room fireplace where we find the next clue hidden underneath a set of andirons. And so it goes. We find the last clue under the thick novel, *The Thorn Birds*, which Rosemary suggested Mom read. Hannah unfolds the paper. "Garret." John and I shrug. "Back to the dictionary!"

"The upper floor; top story," John reads. "Maybe the attic!" We run up, barely touching each landing, dash through Ed's bedroom, and arrive at the attic door in seconds. On the dark wooden treads behind the door to the attic stairs are our prizes: three individually wrapped chocolate MoonPies brought home from Tom's Bar.

ED'S MARRIAGE LASTS FOUR YEARS. After his divorce, he moves in and out of our lives. When in Wheeling, he sleeps in the central bedroom upstairs, a pass-through that we must walk straight through to get to the upstairs bathroom.

I'm bored when Hannah, John, and Ed are all away one evening and decide I'll surprise my oldest brother. I'll clean his room. My heart's in the right place. I dust off his dresser, vacuum the thin carpet, straighten his clothes, and tidy his bed. When I stand back to admire my hard work, it occurs to me I could get back at him for all the tricks he's played on me—the card tricks, the horseplay, and the torturous tickling that made me nearly pee my pants. I decide I'll hide under his bed and wait for him. When he sits on the edge of his bed to remove his shoes and socks, I'll reach out and grab his ankles.

When I hear his car door close outside, I get in place. I scoot on my belly underneath his bed and shimmy back against the wall. He closes the front door and clomps up the stairs. I hear him breathing. I stifle a giggle. He takes off his watch and puts it on the dresser. I imagine he notices how nice his room looks. He goes to the bathroom to pee. When he comes back, he takes off his belt and unbuttons his shirt. I'm holding my breath.

Ed sits on the side of the bed just as I expected he would and removes his shoes.

"Gotcha!" I grab both ankles. He jumps up and screams bloody murder! I'm embarrassed that I've gone to such lengths, but deep, deep down I feel a rare satisfaction. Finally, we are even.

DAD BRAGS that he never gets behind the wheel of a car inebriated. But one summer Saturday, he defies all his principles. After his first big gulp of Old Mr. Boston, Dad lists all the ways he's earned a getaway. Isn't he a dependable, hardworking son of a gun who brings his paychecks home? He announces that he and Mom are taking John and me across the river to Ohio for a picnic with one of Dad's coworkers and his wife. The plan sounds out of character. We never take family outings except for our Cape Cod summer vacations and visits to family. But the weather's nice, and John and I have nothing better to do. Dad's friend has a hunting cabin near Dad's plant and a creek runs nearby. Plus, there will be other kids our age there.

The four of us load up into Mom's four-door and Dad drives us to Ohio, past his plant and over a back road to a cabin that's not too far off the beaten track. Dad introduces us to his coworker, his wife, and the two sons, who are both around John's age.

John and I follow the boys down to the creek to swim. A rope swing hangs from a sturdy tree limb. The boys take turns swinging Tarzan-like over the water and splashing into the creek. I'm on my period. I don't even want to be there, much less swim in this murky, rocky, swimming hole devoid of aquatic life. I perch myself on the bank and tug at my jean cut-offs. The boys seem nice, harmless, and they take turns with John at the rope. They're so different from a gathering of girls. They exhibit an innate sense of belonging. I'm fascinated by how free they are to just be themselves. Are they ever self-conscious about anything? Though they've just met, they laugh and yell and tease each other.

They ignore me, which is a comfort. I wade around in the shallows. When it feels too slimy on my bare feet, I move back to solid ground, sit, and observe. "Aren't you getting in?" John asks me. I shake my head and smile. The two brothers watch for my response. I'm thankful when they resume their play, and I watch them for an hour or so until their mom calls us to the picnic table. She's set out our sandwiches, chips, and sodas and has gone back inside the cabin. After we eat, I wander indoors. I'm shocked at how drunk the adults are after only an hour or so.

We return to the creek until it's time to leave. Dad's in no condition to drive so Mom takes the wheel. Not long after we arrive back home, the phone rings. It's the boys' mom. Dad's coworker has been in an accident. He's in intensive care within inches of losing his life. Our house is quiet with this news. The friend recovers but needs months of rehabilitation. I wonder how his sons are handling it.

Molly and Ed try to intervene in our parents' drinking, pointing out that Mom and Dad have young children at home. But our parents fail to take stock of their unhealthy habits, which have worsened. They are incensed at Molly and Ed. "How dare they? Nobody tells us how to live!" Amid dysfunction and shame, we each grow up the only way we can: by changing the rules to suit ourselves or making them up as we go along. The author Mary Karr describes my psyche when she writes, "The fact that my house was Not Right metastasized into the notion that I myself was Not Right, or that my survival in the world depended on my constant vigilance from various forms of Not Rightness."

SOCIAL LIFE AT ST. MIKE'S occurs in cliques. Without realizing it, I orchestrate a clique faster than Dad can down a shot. My dearest friend, Jess, becomes its scapegoat. All it takes is some negative talk about her behind her back.

It begins when she and I spend countless hours practicing cheerleading on the playground. We meet up after school, too, to practice our jumps, chants, and precision. "Whether we win or whether we lose, this is the cheer we always use: Hey team! Say team! Rah, rah, rah, rah, team!" My gymnastic ability is limited. I'm bottom-heavy and can't get up off the ground during jumps like my friends can. But I never stop trying, and I'm convinced I have to make the squad, an exclusive club. I need to achieve this goal. Wear the uniform.

The summer between our sixth and seventh grades, right before cheerleading tryouts, my friends and I are at a Girl Scout weekend getaway at Camp Giscowheco, near Wheeling. After a fireside break-fast, our leaders leave us to ourselves. We find a small mound of grass for cheerleading practice, especially the part I struggle with the most: jumps. There's a three-foot drop from the grass to the landing beneath it. We take turns doing stunts and jumping down to the landing. The space between the two provides a lofting effect. My jumps are higher than they've ever been. I'm elated when my friends say, "Sarah, you're doing it! You're bound to make it."

I've already done the math: Laura, Janie, Ellen, and Judy will make it. With six spots to fill, there are two spots left for Sheila, Jess, or me. When Sheila and Jess make the squad, I try not to show my disappointment. But I'm crushed. My dreams are shattered. I'm a loser. Mom sees all of this in my tears and my stricken look. She empathizes. But for weeks, I fear that if I'm not good enough for cheerleading, I'm not good enough for anything.

I become a bully. I torture Jess. My other friends and I make her life as miserable as we can. I surprise myself with how easy it is to convince them to shun her. Don't let her sit with us at mass. Don't invite her to sleepovers or to join the circle on the playground when we play games. We laugh at her, exclude her from our slumber parties, and talk about her home as if it's the last place we'd want to be. My cruelty advances unchecked.

> . . . *I take Scotch from my parents' liquor cabinet, conceal it in a tightly lidded container, hide it in the deep, inside pocket of my winter parka and carry it to a friend's party. A few gulps make me dizzy. I pour more. No one joins me, but I'm getting drunk. My friend's older sister notices me slurring my words. Aware of what I'm doing, she takes me to their back porch, sits me down, and talks gently but firmly to me. She says I have to stop right then. For the time being, I do . . .*

Arrested Development

BY MY EARLY TEENS, I'm taking sips of wine at Thanksgiving. The tastes become gulps. I like the dizzy feeling the alcohol gives me.

John is adding inches in height, but he's twenty pounds overweight. Hannah spends most of her time at her friends' houses. We still enjoy the occasional visit with Rosemary, Molly, and their families, but at home the three of us go our separate ways. The experiences that we have no way of talking about continue to accumulate. I don't fully grasp that John is crying out for help. His classmates tease him about his weight. His grades are terrible. The nuns act as if they hate him. Dad's verbal abuse escalates.

John practically lives in his green army jacket. Deep within the front pockets, he hides all sorts of contraband. He smokes cigarettes along with pot; he drinks. Dad harps on John's posture and that his grungy appearance casts a bad name on the family. John's long hair becomes an issue, so John lets it grows longer and longer. At home, John is sullen, and his mood brings me down.

John escapes along Wheeling Creek. There's East Wheeling, South Wheeling, and Edgington Lane—places where he takes cover to use drugs with his friends. The smell of marijuana lingers over him, and his eyes are glassy and red. When I do catch a glimpse of him, John looks like he's carrying a ton of baggage. He's as tall as Dad now, but his eyes shift away, like he's ready to dart the minute somebody looks at him sideways. At home, he retreats to his room. He's hung a life-sized poster of a scantily clad Raquel Welch on the wall above his bed. I check on him occasionally, but I can't get close to him anymore. I resent his drugged state. I resent that he's not interested in anything I do. I sense he wants me to approve of his friends and lifestyle, but he's become a stranger to me. I don't expect him to want to be home with me, but I hate being here alone with Mom and Dad. I withdraw to my room, where I'm left alone.

One night before my thirteenth birthday, my parents are sitting in the kitchen with friends. It's rare for them to entertain. All four are drinking bourbon on ice. I hide in the den, but I'm intrigued by their conversation and laughter. I peek around the corner. Who are these people? Where did Dad meet this guy, who sits up against the wall, and his wife? The man's holding court, telling a long, loud story. He looks like a retired college professor with his white hair slicked back and his round belly underneath his shirt and vest that are kind of dressy for the kitchen table.

On impulse, I walk into the kitchen. "This is our youngest," Dad says. "Isn't she a beauty?" The professor-man makes a low growling sound. I blush. He reaches for me. I think he wants me to shake his hand. Instead, he pulls me in, turns, and inflicts on me a full-blown wet kiss, his tongue like a wet snake in my mouth. I want to throw up! My parents go on talking and laughing, oblivious.

I SPEND HOURS UPSTAIRS on the thin carpet of my floor with a *Seventeen* magazine and a blank, white poster board, scissors, and glue. I'm only fourteen but I look seventeen. I scour the advertising pages and captions of photos for words and phrases that express my angst and my emotional temperature. I cut out words like *far* and *out*. I paste them on the poster board next to individual letters that form phrases like *eat your heart out* or *killing me softly*, from Roberta Flack's song. I mix together characters in all different font sizes, and I hang the collage on my bedroom wall. It resembles a gigantic ransom note with pictures of models thrown in; it's a jumble of images that puts my feelings on paper. Periodically, I open my bedroom door and assess my parents' drinking progression. I know by the clock on the wall if I've waited too long to get their signatures on a paper for school, a permission slip, or a report card. 7:30 p.m.? Too late.

BY NOW, the liquor store clerk knows Mom by name. I hope none of my classmates see me crouching in the back seat while she buys half gallons of Old Grand-Dad bourbon. The parents' relentless routine is predictable: Mom serves us an early supper. She and Dad swagger between the living room where they play cards and the powder room for bathroom breaks. They navigate drunk through the rooms, wobbling like they're on tightropes. Around eight, Mom is in the kitchen trying to reheat dinner for herself and Dad.

It's summer, and I fly on an airplane for the first time, the most thrilling thing I could've imagined. I travel unaccompanied from Pittsburgh to Roanoke, where Molly and her family pick me up. I settle into my seat on the plane wearing my favorite denim jumper along with a blue-and-white-checked blouse. I set my purse under the seat in front of me, buckle up, and listen to the stewardess explain safety protocol as if my life depended on it. "First time to fly?" says the man next to me. "Oh, yes. I'm going to see my sister."

"Nothing to worry about," he says. "I fly every week."

Every seat's filled. Everyone's buckled in. I smile and sit back as the gigantic engines rev up, my heart pounding with anticipation. I look out the window. It's clear and sunny, a great day for my first flight. We taxi to our runway, and I feel as if we passengers are in a deluxe race car. Not like the open-air go-cart that one of our childhood neighbors owned—the one that we used to get in line to ride, the one with the lawn-mower engine that whisked us around Lebanon Manor like we were on our own private figure-8 racetrack. We speed up for takeoff. My heart now pounds from the thrill. Smooth and steady, the plane lifts into the sky. I let out a gasp. The gentleman next to me smiles.

I feel safe, even though I'm strapped into a seventy-five-ton, steel contraption, and the solid earth has disappeared beneath our feet. The seats are more comfortable than I expected; I feel as if I'm seated in someone's living room. I feel so grown-up. The stewardess delivers a soft drink and peanuts. I observe the slender stewardesses in their uniforms and high heels. They all look like contestants for Miss America as they wait on the passengers or offer a small pillow for someone's neck, all the while smiling politely. I make a decision: That's what I'll be! I can perform these tasks.

But if I do become a stewardess, what will happen the first time I'm called upon to open those exit doors? In the event of a crash landing, I'd be ill-equipped, incompetent. Not to mention the drinking games I'd play. Having access to all those tiny, easy-to-hide bottles, I'd be a disaster in the making.

I have no idea what I actually want to be, but I'm certain I want to have kids. Babysitting has convinced me I'm pretty good with little ones. As for work, I can shine Dad's shoes and deliver John's newspapers. When I empty Mrs. Dreyfus's trash, sweep her floors, and straighten her bed, she pays me five dollars. But, I don't understand what it means to have a career outside the home. Mom seems well suited for homemaking, and I will be too.

IN AUGUST 1974, Molly takes me to Long Beach, North Carolina, with her family, and I listen to the radio as Richard Nixon resigns the presidency. But, the tropical storm that sweeps through that night has a far greater impact on my fifteen-year-old self. I hyperventilate all night with fear that our rickety beach-front cottage will implode.

Molly has established a career in nursing, and I can listen for hours as she talks about our family dynamics and about her patients in the hospital. She never names names, but she recalls every detail of a night spent monitoring someone close to death in the intensive care unit. I'm so impressed by her ability to handle life-and-death situations that I end up entering nursing school after I graduate high school. I don't stick with nursing, but I still want to emulate Molly's self-assurance.

Molly remains a positive influence in my life. She and Robby raise two children. Their daughter, with curly blonde pigtails, follows me everywhere and asks me endless questions, especially when I become a teenager. Their son is quiet but sweet. They live not far from where our family once lived. When I fly down to visit one summer, we drive past our old house in Lebanon Manor. It looks teeny-tiny compared to our Wheeling home. We drive to Robby's mother's house where Molly does her mother-in-law's hair and her own. No beauty parlors for these women. Molly's brought curlers, bobby pins, and setting gel. She lines them up on the kitchen table. I've never been privy to the world where a married woman hangs out with her older and wiser mother-in-law. I can't imagine our mom and Granny spending an afternoon helping each other with such intimate grooming.

IT'S FRIDAY NIGHT. John and I are fifteen and fourteen. It's one of the rare Fridays when Mom and Dad have gone out to dinner—at the Rose Café, a long drive from home. I go skating, and when I get home afterwards, the lights are dim and I smell pot. John and his buddies are sitting on the floor in the TV room; the only light is from the glare of the TV. In the dim glow, I can see they're all smiling, as they pass around a joint. There's a thick marijuana haze. "Come join us!" they say when they realize I'm John's sister. This is the first time I join in John's pot-smoking and, afterwards, he warns me: "Sarah, I better never hear of you using anything stronger than pot, especially the psychedelic stuff. I know you.

You couldn't handle it." As if he could. But I remember the warning and his serious look. I don't go there.

That fall, Ed takes us out of school for a day in Washington, DC. He has a job interview with the Library of Congress. He takes us first to Georgetown, where every shop has something for hippies: tie-dyed skirts and scarves, love beads, and peace signs. Later, Ed turns us loose for several hours while he goes to his interview. It's an intoxicating freedom; we stroll the wide sidewalks down Pennsylvania Avenue. John suggests we find ice cream, which we do in a small indoor mall under the Watergate Hotel.

We're mesmerized by a scene that unfolds before our eyes. Two well-dressed politicians are descending the steps of a large office building. Paparazzi are speeding up the steps, two at a time, towards them, trying to block the men with their huge cameras and equipment. Other news reporters are carrying microphones, and they thrust them in the politicians' faces as they try to negotiate the steps and avoid the cameras. While all of this is taking place, we hear voices yelling at the politicians from high atop scaffolding. The hard hats are making megaphones with their hands. "You're going to jail!"

When John and I tell Ed about the drama, he explains the scandal of Watergate. We've just seen H. R. Haldeman and John Ehrlichman, the former president Richard Nixon's men. Driving back to Wheeling, Ed pulls out a pipe and offers John a smoke. They inhale deeply, and Ed looks over at me in the front passenger seat.

"Ever smoke pot?" he asks.

"Yeah, one night with John and his friends in the den. Didn't feel anything, though."

"Here," he says. "Draw in the smoke and hold it a second before exhaling." So I do. After a few hits, Ed starts telling us about his job interview. When he's done, I realize I haven't been able to follow him, though the sound of his voice and the way he speaks sound really intelligent.

"Ed, tell me that whole story one more time." He cracks up, laughing at his young sister, the pothead.

EMILY IS THE VERY BEST THING that happens to me at St. Mike's. We're in eighth grade. Her father had died suddenly, and the family relocated to Wheeling from New Jersey. I spy her from across the playground. She stands all alone. She has long, blonde hair and looks more developed, like me. She's not skinny or flat chested. Both of us at fourteen can pass easily for sixteen.

I gather the nerve to introduce myself. She tells me her father died from an aneurism, whatever that is, when he was only thirty-five. She doesn't cry. She can talk about it. She has a younger brother and two younger sisters. I figure she grew up fast. She and her family have relatives in Wheeling, so here they are. They live close by on Poplar Avenue. "That's my neighborhood," I say. Should I just take my chances and invite her over? I'd burned some bridges with my school friends, but she's new. She doesn't yet know me, my family, my faults. We can start fresh, see how compatible we are. She becomes for me what Anna is to Hannah. Those two laugh so easily with each other and are inseparable.

Emily and I click, but I really don't want to blow it. I invite her to come over, and I mentally rehearse how to prepare her. Our house is filled with second-hand smoke. My parents drink a lot. They act ridiculous. And we have this insane walk-through powder room, between the kitchen and den, that has two doors. Don't ever sit down to pee in there before locking both doors, or someone will walk in on you. It's seldom clean. The entire house is pretty disgusting.

She must like my condescending attitude. She smiles and accepts the invitation. I go straight home. She'll be here after I clean and before my parents start slurring their words.

When she arrives, I introduce her to my parents. We go to my room and talk as if we've known each other for years. James Taylor sings,

"Hey, ain't it good to know that you've got a friend?"

"My parents are so sickening," I say. "They're not so bad," Emily says. "Trust me. Not compared to my mom. She stays in bed a lot. Her doctor gave her some pills." From that afternoon on, we're inseparable.

Emily is well read. I catch up so we can talk about the classics. She's even saved money for her own stereo. We have the same taste in music, in boys, and in our disdain for our respective home lives. Emily's mom is devastated over the sudden loss of her husband and being left to raise her four children alone. *So what if she takes to bed*, I think.

Emily says her mom is being consoled by a dear friend who later becomes her serious boyfriend and, eventually, her husband. Vinnie hails from New York and is a most genial Italian man, with curly black hair and a Carlos Santana look. He visits Emily's mom and her family most every weekend. "Guess who's coming this weekend?" Emily whispers to me from her desk across the aisle in Sister Teresa's classroom.

"Vinnie?" I smile. He'll bring pastries from his family's bakery in Jersey City. "You know that wedding scene, the reception in *The Godfather* movie?" Emily asks. "Notice the tall wedding cake? It was made at Vinnie's family's bakery." Having Vinnie around is like having a New York City celebrity in our midst. He's vibrant, talkative, and charming. He's a light in that sometimes dark home. And he takes special interest in not just Emily, but in me too, like I'm one of the family. Emily and I trust him.

THAT YEAR, I'm asked to take the lead in my eighth grade's school musical variety show. Some local thespians associated with the famed Oglebay Institute's theater created the show to honor a retiring priest—a beloved rector from St. Mike's parish. I dress like a nun for my two-night performance. In my part, I prompt the other actors, my fellow students, to tell jokes and to sing solos and duets. I also sing a solo, "Kids!" My friend and often coconspirator T.J. also sings a solo, "King of the Road."

Rehearsals are held after school for weeks. One of the nuns calls me out one day for a costume fitting. I follow her across the street to the convent. We don't speak a word. My palms sweat when I anticipate entering the nuns' private space. She escorts me into an austere bedroom that's furnished with nothing but a single bed, a hard-backed chair, and a small table with a lamp. A crucifix hangs over the bed. The nun tells me she wants me to put on the habit—a full-length, long-sleeved, white shift with a full-length black apron. A white rope belt, a long crucifix necklace, and a stiff headpiece complete the look. She leaves me to sort it out and says she'll be right back. There are no mirrors. When she returns, she fits the headpiece on me and admires her expertise. "You look just like one of our new novices," she says, in a sappy voice. Now I know how Maria felt in *Sound of Music*. "No, Reverend Mother! I can't!"

As Mom and I leave the house on the first night of our production, Dad wishes me luck. I accept that he can't—and won't—be in public without a drink in hand. Especially at St. Mike's.

The show is sold out. Mom remains somewhere in the back of the dark auditorium. Her presence neither adds nor detracts from my nerves or my expectations. Our kind neighbor Mr. Alexander is in the audience, and I play to the crowd. The show is a big hit. I receive accolades for my role as the nun and for my solo. The older crowd seems especially pleased.

After the final performance the next night, some of the kids in the show invite me to join them at Elby's for a celebratory meal. I politely turn down their invitation, follow Mom through the parking lot, and get in the passenger seat. "Sarah, you were terrific tonight. You sure you don't want to join your friends?" she asks.

"Oh, no. Just take me home." What is going on in my head? It's one of the best nights of my life. Never before have so many people told me how wonderful my performance was. I even fooled some folks into believing I actually was a nun! Afterward, I want the seclusion of my bedroom to process what has happened. For days, I receive more praise and gifts: flowers, cards, and letters, including one from a woman who directed our local theater troupe. "Sarah—you must pursue the stage. You have natural talent. Oglebay Institute is here for you." My confidence soars, and my social life develops a nice flow.

AT CHRISTMAS TIME, our tree stands in the corner of the living room adorned with colorful lights and silver icicles. In the kitchen, Mom's homemade fruitcake sits atop the refrigerator, shrouded by a rum-laden cheesecloth that makes the entire first floor smell like a distillery. Dad is known to reach under the corner of the damp cloth, pinch off a piece, and swoon. The most exciting moment is when I receive new white ice skates fitted with shiny steel blades and free of scuffs.

I ice-skate with friends at Wheeling Park's White Palace. The rink becomes our rehearsal stage for high school. Our parents take turns carpooling. Mom's always glad to fill her station wagon with pubescent girls who chat nonstop and sing along with the radio at the top of their lungs. When she looks at me in the rearview mirror, I feel safely ensconced. I sing along lustily. "If you don't know me by now, you will never, never, never know me."

The White Palace skating rink provides respite from everything that bothers me. Carefully lacing up both sides of the leather skates becomes a favorite ritual. I become adept at crisscrossing the long laces, pulling them through the hooks, tightening the strings just so around my ankles and calves, and then tying a big bow. I cannot wait to get out on the ice. I never fall. I can skate backwards and do figure eights.

Most of the sixth, seventh, and eighth graders come to the ice rink on Friday nights, as do the older teens. Occasionally I see John with his friends, all wearing green army jackets. Their heads are covered by knit toboggans, and their big feet sport the rented, black ice skates. John likes the girls in his class, and they like him. During the couples skates, he glides by with a sweet and pretty ninth-grader. "How you gettin' home?" I ask him as I skate nearby. He and his partner smile at me. This John is not the same John as the John I live with. "Don't worry about me, Salou." I wave him off, dig my blades in deeper, and speed away.

Students from other schools come to the Friday skate too. Eighth grade Catholic classes from the different schools all merge for ninth grade every fall, so these boys and girls from Elm Grove's St. Vincent's Elementary School, from Warwood's Corpus Christi, from East Wheeling, Bethlehem, and North Wheeling will be classmates at Wheeling Central Catholic High School. Many are second generation immigrants from Lebanon, Italy, and Greece. Our cliques are thrown into a recycling machine. We all become friends.

If my young, teenage world needs an outlet for showmanship, friendships, and excitement, those three hours on the ice rink with piped-in organ music provide it. We don't care that the music isn't the Top 40. We revel in the open-air ice-dancing and the races we spontaneously hold as light snowflakes fall under a dark winter sky. Sometimes we skate in pairs and hold hands. Other times we all hold hands to form a long whip. The lead skater sets a fast pace and whips the tail of skaters off in another direction once they let go. I chase boys with abandon after they steal the tasseled hat off my head and race away. The boys can skate ridiculously fast. They'll rise early on Saturday for hockey practice. Ice-skating is exhilarating. The cold wind on my cheeks and forehead stimulates me. I feel free. My thick thighs grow strong, along with my ankles that are also thick—like Granny's, whose ankles rolled over the tops of her shoes.

Every hour, a man announces over the loud speaker. "Fifteen-minute break." We race to the edge as the giant ice-smoothing machine, three times the size of a John Deere, glides onto the rink and erases all evidence of our blades. I hold on to the railing, depart the ice area, and march carefully on my thin blades to the rubber-floored waiting area. I clomp across it with a stop-and-start motion, aiming for the concession stand and blistering hot chocolate. We sit on benches with friends and catch our breath. Our head and ear coverings are vital parts of our winter wardrobes. Instead of jeans or a sweater, I ask Mom for new earmuffs or a new knit hat with a pom-pom that's easy for Donnie, Tom, or Paul to snatch as they skate by.

With the announcements that all can now skate again, we race back to the ice. We skate until the Couples Only announcement. I traipse back to the sides and try not to get caught checking for a boy who might invite me to skate. I wait to hear the All Skate announcement and then run back onto the ice, dig my blades into the surface, and get a long slide going.

Each time we skate around the oval, we pass the parents, all hatted and scarfed, lined up along a ramp keeping track of their children and their children's friends. Occasionally I see Hannah's friends, who don't like to skate. If I spy one of the really cute guys from Hannah's class checking me out, I make a quick exit for the restroom, check my appearance in the mirror before returning refreshed, ready to hold my head up high on the frozen stage. In a few years, I'll be on a different stage, representing my class as homecoming maid, escorted by my dad, who will be even more nervous than me.

. . . My family raises no eyebrows when I drink at Thanksgiving and Christmas, and I slowly but surely stumble into an alcoholic mindset. Drinking serves two purposes: it makes me feel a part of my family, and it gets me drunk. At first, I like fitting in. Holding the glass, I believe I'm more sophisticated. The drug takes effect, and I relax. I lose all inhibitions. Gulp after gulp, my mind gives in to oblivion. So, this is how it feels to be an adult, I think.

One evening, after the parents are asleep, Ed brings home a party girl. She and I drink all the liquor that's on the kitchen counter, polishing off the numerous mostly empty bottles. I try gin for the first time. I remember we sat on the floor facing each other, and after falling backwards a few times, I spring back up. I barely recall Ed helping me upstairs to bed . . .

It's All About the Pit Crew

IN THE SUMMER OF 1975, Hannah is living in Texas with her new husband, who's in the air force, and their new baby girl. So, this time it's just Mom, Dad, John, and I for a two-week vacation trip at a new beach. Our parents have switched their allegiance from Cape Cod (too far) to the Maryland shore. Ed even makes a visit to Ocean City to see us. I enjoy way too much freedom, going out with three different young men (total strangers).

I don't consider myself promiscuous, but I test the waters. My last night at the beach, Mom and Dad send John to look for me. Imagine him being the responsible one! He finds me with a lifeguard—making out in our parents' car.

I hear John's hard knock on the window. I'm startled and jerk away from the heavy petting. "Sarah! Get inside the cottage. Mom and Dad sent me looking for you. It's time to come in!" he says, through the foggy window.

I return home to Wheeling with a glow of new sexual exploits, but my virginity and self-esteem are intact, thanks to John. He never makes me feel bad about myself, but he teases me about being boy crazy.

John actually remains behind in Ocean City. Our parents give him permission to stay and live with new friends, and to work at Lombardo's Pizza Shop the rest of the summer. While he's in Maryland, we write back and forth. I bake him a few dozen chocolate chip cookies, and Mom helps me package them up to send to him. I receive a chatty thank-you.

"Gee, Salou, thanks so much for the cookies. That was awfully nice of you. I'd have eaten more of them, but one of the girls here at the house found them, and before I knew it, they were all gone." That's when I realize he's staying in a house with multiple people. He tells me about the beautiful sunsets he's enjoying. When he makes reference to some "really good drugs," I know the beauty of the beach is being masked behind his drug-induced haze.

JUST DAYS AFTER JOHN RETURNS to Wheeling, on the Sunday of Labor Day weekend, my brother, parents, and I find ourselves in a disaster so out of control, it catches us completely off guard.

We don't go to church that rainy, sticky day; we have pretty much given up on weekly mass attendance by then. John's appearance is really different. He has lost twenty-five pounds. While we are lazing around watching TV, Mom and Dad are in the living room, reading the Sunday paper. It has rained practically nonstop the entire week.

Our phone rings, breaking into our quiet morning like an alarm. It's our next-door neighbor calling, asking for Dad. She's calling from southern West Virginia, not from her home; she's heard reports of severe weather—flash floods—in our area. I hear Dad say, "Yes, we've had a lot of rain, but . . .," and the next thing I know, he places the phone down and races for the back door.

"Viola is concerned about our cars," Dad yells to Mom on his way out. He's been renting space from Viola. His work car is parked next to hers in her garage, which is right next to the alley adjacent to the creek. Our one-car garage can only accommodate Mom's green Ford station wagon.

When Dad finds the small creek directly across from our home filled to the brim with floodwater, he runs back indoors. Dad grabs the phone and tells Viola, "I'm going now to try to save our cars!" His voice is an octave higher. He's panic-stricken. The very moment Dad goes to rescue the cars, the swelling water begins pouring over the creek's retaining wall.

When John and I hear Dad's plan, we run to our front window to see for ourselves. Floodwaters are taking over our side and front yards. A cappuccino-colored river bulges with whitecaps.

There's no time to think. Mom stands at the window with us, trembling, "Oh, my God!"

"We have to get out now, Mom!" John says.

Her head shakes. "I can't just leave!" She's suddenly frail in her thin housecoat. She appears incapable of leaving under her own power, so John and I get on either side of her. But it's as if her feet are stuck to the carpet. We practically force her to take baby steps out onto the front porch. By that time, our garage is starting to break away from the house. The wood cracking and snapping under the water's force sounds like having a sea monster tearing our house apart.

John jerks open our heavy front door. The water is rising up our front porch steps. We have to get Mom down the five wooden treads before we lose our footing. A neighbor sees our plight and wades down the street in waist-deep water to help us with her. We make it to solid ground, about a hundred feet up from the floodwaters.

We all just stand there, watching the spectacle and listening to crashing debris pulled along in the raging creek. Mom is moaning and crying.

Dad comes hurrying from behind the next-door neighbor's property. He was able to save the two cars. He puts his arm around Mom, and the two of them just stand there in the pouring rain, staring with the rest of us. In seconds flat, our garage detaches from the house, its green, cedar siding torn apart in loud screeches. Fragments drift away swiftly, followed by Mom's station wagon.

That car, which I'd often borrowed from Mom, floats out into our front yard and gets stuck, held in place by a large elm tree. The steel body bobs up and down in a menacing way and is about to be swallowed up. After three or four crashes against the tree, the hood buckles hideously. The vehicle has become a total loss in a demolition derby by Mother Nature. In an instant, both the garage and car float rapidly away.

Suddenly, the water recedes. John and I wonder, *what destruction awaits us in our home?* I become convinced the house's foundation is compromised. None of us is ready to go back indoors to investigate. Mom's still trembling.

The four of us enter the house.

A thick, acrid mud covers the once-green carpet in the living room. The entire first floor is silty brown. The bases of Dad's tall grandfather clocks are filled with sludge. Their beautiful wood cases are marked by a water line thirteen inches up from the floor. When he carefully ventures to the top of the basement stairs and looks down, Dad begins to weep.

The heavy, upright freezer that had been directly at the bottom of the stairs is nowhere in sight. Dad later finds it upside down in another basement room. His antique clock parts and tools are strewn everywhere. Even the washer and dryer are missing.

Family and friends descend on our home in droves for weeks afterward. Personally, I hope the engineer who comes to inspect the cracked cinder blocks of the foundation will label the home "unsafe." I want out. I think we should leave, not stay. Our neighbors are all very fortunate. The way our house is perched at the very end—the low end—of a sloping street, it is the only house to take the brunt of the flood's devastation.

For days, the basement and first floor smell like a mix of stagnant creek bed and dead fish. The second story, by contrast, is as dry and clean as it ever was, and that's where I choose to stay most of the time. Electricity is out for a week, and the house becomes deeply dark at night.

Ed, John, and their friends, plus our brother-in-law Robby and sister Molly, help with the laborious work necessary to fix up the downstairs. They tear out the carpets, hose off the floors, and remove drywall. They open up the basement hatch adjacent to our driveway to access the ruined appliances. They haul everything out and make a huge pile of debris. It's blistering hot. The friends are all shirtless and in cut-off jeans. They wear bandanas tied around their heads and necks to catch the sweat, like a hippie pit crew. That's when I really notice how much John has changed.

Earlier that summer, he'd been carrying close to two hundred pounds on his six-foot-two frame. The young man who came back from Ocean City at the end of summer, when I finally paid attention, had trimmed down, was tan, and had maybe even grown another inch. My now-lanky brother is different but more than just physically. He fits in with all of the energetic men working tirelessly on clearing out the debris. Shovels in hand, they rarely pause from the backbreaking work. An army of long-haired West Virginians, those men get down and dirty in that creek to clear away, by hand, the web of gnarly branches, tree limbs, and thick trunks.

Neighbors carry in food and express sympathy. Though nobody died, grief is in the air. I overeat, feeling so sorry for myself and our parents.

Starting the new school year is a reprieve from the nasty smells of the catastrophe. It takes months before we see real progress in restoring the house from all the damage. Mom and Dad are able to secure a low-interest government loan since they have no flood insurance.

WHILE THE HOUSE is still undergoing the necessary cleaning, it starts to storm again late one afternoon. Dad's been drinking heavily since noon. The workers have all left for the day. Family stands around in the kitchen taking a break from all of the emotional and physical stress of discarding so many ruined treasures. Dad keeps stepping out onto the back porch stoop, watching the sky as it turns dark. The wind increases as a hard rain falls into the creek. Dad reports on the threatening weather, his new enemy. At least he isn't taking the situation out on John this time.

When debris washes down from the runs and tributaries of the upper reaches of Oglebay Park, it's supposed to flow through pipes and feed into Wheeling Creek. Eventually, it arrives at the Ohio River. But now, those pipes are getting clogged again. After all the work our crew has done, the unusually thick logjam is once again preventing the waters from heading in their proper direction. We all become concerned. The water in the creek is rising.

Dad's anger takes him to the phone where he calls the governor's office to complain at the top of his inebriated lungs about the lack of maintenance on the creek. He's getting nowhere with the authorities, so he decides to take things in his own hands. He marches upstairs to the attic and comes back down with his loaded rifle.

He grabs the screen door forcefully and heads out to the back porch, raising the weapon in a Moses-like gesture, signaling battle. He threatens both the creek and the sky, claiming he can "shoot the clouds!" In his mind, he'll trigger some meteorological mechanism to "stop the damn rain!"

I freeze. My heart races with the sound of his thundering voice, sensing how powerless we all are, yet again, to stop the forces of Mother Nature and to stop our dad.

Mom, Molly, and Ed frantically talk him out of firing the weapon. He lowers the rifle, and he and Mom both have a cry. I'm worn out from the scene, back out of the kitchen, and run upstairs to my room. Still no electricity, I seek refuge under a flashlight and turn the pages of a *Seventeen* magazine. I'm not really reading, but just grateful Dad saw the wisdom in putting the gun away.

I hate living in our stinky house. I become resentful having a house full of people day and night, even if it is family. School's resumed and

I want to get on with my social life, but I've eaten way too much cake from all the neighbors who brought food. My uniform is dreadfully tight. As a sixteen-year-old becoming obsessed with my appearance, I'm just plain miserable.

The bright spot is seeing John hold it together. Spending those summer weeks away in Ocean City was a brilliant move. No longer is he my wayward brother; John has a new air of confidence and independence. His help in cleaning out after the flood even garners a handshake from Dad. What he's lost in weight, he's gained in respect. John tries out for the wrestling team. With his lengthening torso and his long legs and arms, he's a natural. On weekends, he wanders around with new friends who enjoy the same things he does. John's popularity with his friends skyrockets. He's dating new girls and living what appears to be a more peaceful life. From that point on, he's seldom home.

... I drink now on all major holidays, special occasions, long weekends, and all days ending in Y. Early on, it doesn't affect my friendships, but I gravitate towards girls my age who also like to drink. We sneak around, guzzle the heavy stuff, and steal from our parents' liquor cabinets. I meet Deidra and Rona at the ball field. We chug the liquid until it no longer burns. My friend Teresa doesn't know. I become two different people, depending on who I'm with.

I never carry enough alcohol to hurt myself, and I'm always on foot, so I am able to practically sober up by the time I arrive home. Carrying contraband makes me feel a bit risky, and certainly older. When I'm sixteen, I begin barhopping. I'm never carded ...

IV

Under the Influence

HIGH SCHOOL HAS BECOME a place where I develop a sense of belonging. Emily and I remain best friends, but we also enjoy hanging out with different groups. Having Hannah and John there before me has laid out a kind of welcome mat, and I'm thrilled when recognized by their friends, the older classmates, who stop me in the hallway to say hello. Like Hannah, I make pretty good grades, do community service projects, attend all the dances, and become involved in dramatics as well as speech and debate. I date a popular football player named David, who is a good kisser and has a great sense of humor. I enjoy attending his games and shouting the cheers with the pep club. When basketball season rolls around, we all meet downtown at the high school gym, where we peel off our knitted scarves and coats inside the warm enclosure, take a seat on the bleachers and enjoy giving our spectator support to our beloved Maroon Knights. I develop a strong connection to my classmates, and we often make plans to meet up in large groups after a game—at a bonfire out at the creek or at one of the parks.

MOM, DAD, AND I DRIVE to Abingdon, Virginia, for New Year's Eve. This visit is different from so many other Abingdon visits: I'm on my own. John is staying with friends, and while Mom and Dad are there the entire time, I experience complete independence from them on this trip. They're out visiting some of Rosemary's friends, a list of names that Rosemary handed Dad upon our arrival. It's good friends of hers who've asked them over so Dad can repair their clocks on site. They've all become quite chummy after years of sitting across from each other at Rosemary's card table, playing bridge.

In the past, at our sister's, John and I were expert at making ourselves scarce. We had a clear but unspoken message from our parents, "We love you, but go away." Even when Rosemary and Geoffrey lived in Virginia Beach, before they moved to Abingdon, John and I found ways to avoid the adults. We were thick as thieves and good at lying low.

We looked after ourselves. I remember once when John and I were walking down to the beach on a windy asphalt road that went downhill a long, long way. We got hot, and John put out his thumb at the first sign of a car. Hitchhiking was in vogue. A four-door car pulled over, and John opened the back door for me. Nothing about the driver reminded me of the pervert in the hatchback. I got in. John sat beside me. "To the beach," John said, as if he was giving orders to our own personal chauffeur. The man drove us to the end of the road and dropped us off.

This holiday stay in Abingdon goes in an entirely different direction. It's just me. I miss my accomplice, but not having my parents about much makes me lighthearted. Plus, Rosemary and Geoffrey have just returned from traveling through Europe and are still exhilarated.

I enjoy being around Rosemary. Her interests and passions are many. How she loves visiting Key West: the ocean, the artists, the sunsets. She is fun-loving, gregarious, and sociable. Everywhere she has lived, she is warm and welcoming to people from all walks of life. And, she cooks grand meals for friends and newcomers. When we arrive, Rosemary's preparing for the big bash she's hosting that evening.

Her life is as glamorous as anyone's I can imagine—rich in experiences, books, intellectual friends, and travels. She has such command of her kitchen, extracting grease-stained copies of *Bon Appétit* magazines from a handy shelf in her brick kitchen. As she cooks, she nurses a drink. I follow her from room to room as she sets out candles and assembles food platters in the kitchen. "Grab that bottle opener in the third drawer," she tells me, as she sets out an impressive display of wine and liquor. "Did you bring anything special to wear tonight?" she asks with a gleam in her eyes.

I nod, glad to be with my classy sister. She's already dressed in a stylish, low-cut maxi dress. Her clothes always match her bohemian lifestyle to a T. "I've arranged another date for you with Gabe," she says, smiling. "Hope you don't mind. He wants to take you to a New Year's Eve bash across town."

"Not at all. Sounds great!" I trust her matchmaking skills. Her best friend's son is friends with John, and John, like Rosemary, had suggested I meet Gabe. I certainly clicked with the handsome guy, who will be a student at William & Mary soon. Last summer, the two of us had gone to an Eagles concert. "He'll pick you up around nine," Rosemary adds.

I spend most of the afternoon getting ready. I fix my long hair to look its best—sweeping over my shoulders and curled on the ends. I pay special attention to my eye makeup. I use a little lip gloss. I'd even brought a necklace and earrings to go with my new rust-colored velvety jumpsuit with its matching belt. When I descend my sister's staircase in the clingy outfit that accentuates my curves, the guests at the bottom of Rosemary's stairs turn to watch me. They smile and say things that make me feel beautiful.

My sister's library and parlor overflow with all types. Her guests look so sophisticated with fancy drinks in their hands. The partners from Geoffrey's firm wear suits. The man who owns coal mines wears overalls; the senator from Richmond wears suspenders. Several actors from the Barter Theater wear jeans. Rosemary's best friends are decked out in stylish maxi dresses. Their attention gives me a rush. My heart races with the same nervous excitement I felt when I was on stage. But this feels like a rite of passage with me as the debutante. I smile graciously at all the compliments. "Rosemary, your sister is gorgeous. Prettier than you!" one man says. Then, the front door opens wide, the late December wind pours in, and my handsome date whisks me off to another party.

These memories of Abingdon are sealed forever in my heart. I was born and came of age in these Virginia Highlands.

BACK HOME, the phone rings one day after school, and it's Emily. She's talking so fast, I tell her to slow down.

"I said, go ask your parents if you can come with me on the class trip to Europe over Easter break. There's one slot left, and you can take it!"

"Wait," I say. "Isn't this your French class? I'm taking Spanish."

"I know," she says, "but I asked permission for you and they said yes. Now, go ask!" So, I do, and my parents do not hesitate for one second to allow me to go. The prospect of their practically having the house all to themselves for over a week is too much to pass up. Mom takes me shopping for an outfit to wear on the plane. The day of our departure, she snaps a photo of us on our way to the airport.

Emily and I enjoy the trip of a lifetime—both of us are so enthusiastic. Seeing London with our own eyes; attending Easter services in a small, English chapel; viewing the White Cliffs of Dover as our boat rides across the English Channel; and arriving in romantic Paris where we tour the Notre Dame and Versailles. The memories we make traipsing around Europe cement our friendship even further.

NOT LONG AFTER EMILY AND I RETURN from our trip, John announces that Gabe and his family have moved to Sewickley, Pennsylvania, an hour's drive from Wheeling. I'm intrigued. I figure he's dating other girls, but after he wrote me a heartfelt letter, I knew we'd remain friends. "He wants us to come spend the weekend," John says. "He said you can bring a friend if you want. He wants to take us out on his sailboat."

I call Emily right away and tell her everything. "You game?" She is. That weekend, John drives us to the picturesque countryside north of the Pittsburgh airport. We follow Gabe's directions and find their home. We pull up the driveway. An enormous silo stands on the side of a three-story, modernized farmhouse. Emily's jaw drops at the sight.

Gabe greets us with a hug and, for John, a handshake. "So glad you're here." I introduce Gabe to Emily. "Very cool house," she says. John and I agree.

"This used to be a working farm with stables. The silo is divided into three levels now."

The interior of the house has an ultramodern, open floor plan with multiple levels running off the kitchen and family room. Gabe's mom, sister, and brother greet us before they depart for a tennis lesson. Gabe opens the door to a breezeway. At the end of the walkway, we're surprised to see the house has its own gymnasium. We stand on a balcony above a large basketball court that was once a stable. We then tour the silo, accessing each level by a spiral staircase. The first floor is a charming powder room; the middle level is a library encased with floor-to-ceiling, rounded bookshelves. The top floor, a glass observatory, overlooks the estate.

Gabe shows Emily and me to the guest room where we'll sleep. After dinner, we sit on the patio and plan the next day. "There's a lake nearby where I can take my sailboat. Weather should be perfect tomorrow."

The next morning, John helps Gabe hitch the boat trailer to his vehicle. Gabe's mom has packed a cooler full of cold soft drinks and sandwiches. Emily and I privately assess our situation. "Can you believe all of this?" I say.

"Gabe is as cool as you said he was. Gorgeous too!" Emily says. "This may be the most awesome weekend we've ever had!" The four of us are in sync. John, Emily, and I have never sailed. We follow Gabe's lead on every move and listen carefully to his instructions. Once we leave the shore, Gabe proves adept with the sails and tiller. Emily and I duck when Gabe warns: "Watch the boom!"

Changing direction in a sailboat demands quick adjustments, and I encounter the long wooden bar that crosses above our heads when we come about. We laugh and catch the perfect breeze on those smooth waters. The day is sunny and the motion lulls us into a blissful state. Hundreds of yards from other boaters, we feel we have the lake all to ourselves.

John pulls out a large joint laced with hashish. We all smoke. A mellow tranquility comes over us. We eat a leisurely lunch and occasionally someone tells a joke that makes us laugh hysterically. I remember that too-good-to-be-true day fondly. It was the last day any of us hang out with Gabe. He and his family move to Australia, and we lose touch. Years later, I see his mom and sister who tell me Gabe is happily married and successful.

DRINKING A GLASS OF WINE or a mixed drink lets me feel grown-up. I've been imbibing hard liquor since I was fourteen, the summer Rosemary mixed me my first vodka and orange juice during one of my family's twice-yearly trips to see her. She and Geoffrey, quite noticeably, begin to be at odds. During my last visit, I find myself in the middle of their arguing. On his way outdoors to play tennis, my brother-in-law stops in his tracks when he finds his wife and me out on their front porch relaxing. I sense the tension right away, and he begins picking away at her about her appearance.

"Aren't you going to fix that wild hair today?" he says, his tone of voice condescending. Rosemary smooths out her hair, frizzy from the humidity. She shrugs off his comment, and I sit there cringing. Is he serious? The air is thick with tension. I'm suddenly planning not to stay any longer.

By this time, it's a given: Rosemary drinks and plays cards all day. I never see Geoffrey drunk, and he seems preoccupied with work. There's talk of breaking up. I, along with their two young children, am devastated when they separate and divorce. In the years to come, Rosemary's eyes turn yellow. Her stomach becomes quite distended. As our family watches her decline, none of us believe we can do anything at all about it.

LEFT TO OUR OWN DEVICES, Hannah, John, and I view it all through our developing, teenage lenses and want only to survive what is going on. When we come upon our parents making out on the couch, we fly upstairs—where *they* should be. We have too much time on our hands and no supervision or structure after school. I act out at school. I pass notes in class; I'm mean to some girls on the playground. I get in trouble with the nuns. If Dad knew, he'd come unglued, and Dad's wrath scares me more than that of the nuns. When Hannah's a senior at Central Catholic, she gets pregnant and marries her boyfriend.

Wheeling's loose about underage drinking. The history of our city includes gangsters, open gambling, and authorities who look the other way. William "Big Bill" Lias became a bootlegger at thirteen and ran the town until he was convicted on charges of tax evasion. But he was acquitted and became manager of the Downs Race Track. Lias was a local hero despite his criminal activity and the twenty-six brothels he owned down on the river, which housed notorious women such as Alma Henderson. Wheeling's past sets the tone. Underage drinking is commonplace.

One evening, Ed says, "Get dressed. I'm taking you out." That means he's taking his sixteen-year-old sister to his favorite bar. I take extra time with my long hair: I curl, separate, and tightly wrap it around two large empty orange juice cans. Once it's dry, I unveil the Farrah Fawcett style. I wear my best bell-bottom jeans, a cropped top, and hoop earrings.

At Ed's hangout, I meet his drinking buddies. I perch on a barstool and pose as if I'm on display. If Ed hadn't ordered me a coke, I would have had a beer right along with him. I glow from the conversations with several men who sit on the other side of me, naïve to their one-liners. Ed listens and gets a kick out of the attention I receive. I feel like I'm rehearsing for somebody else's play—performing for what, I'm not sure. Ed never leaves my side. I wonder, *What would Hannah think of me now?* I begin to really miss her, and our late night talks. I can't quite keep track of her these days . . . Ohio, then Texas, while her husband is in US Air Force training.

A week later, Ed moves away. I write him a long letter, pouring out my angst at John and I being the last ones at home under the parents' microscope. Mom and Dad have endured Ed's divorce, Hannah's teenage pregnancy, Rosemary's divorce, and Molly's bout with severe Crohn's Disease.

Finally, John is caught selling pot. The student buyer has nodded off in class. The dean of discipline and the principal find out why, which doesn't sit well. Our parents have to come to the school for a meeting. Though John is expelled, my parents are uncharacteristically supportive of him when he says other students who commit such infractions are allowed to remain. John has their attention though. When they try to confront his marijuana use in front of the authorities, he challenges them. "If you want me to quit smoking pot, then the two of you need to stop drinking." Nobody wins that contest.

John doesn't miss a beat after being expelled. He already has friends at Triadelphia, the public high school. He's a handsome, blue-eyed, six-foot-two, curly haired charmer. He enrolls immediately and graduates the next year with kids his own age. He returns to Central one last time to escort the senior homecoming queen at halftime of the football game. He enjoys accompanying her onto the field and being cheered by his former classmates.

I've become quite covert. My wayward siblings have raised the bar. My parents expect a lot of me, and I feel their scrutiny. I write to Ed, and

I receive an encouraging letter in response. "Everything's going to be okay. Mom and Dad are just a bit shell-shocked. And don't you worry; when they had you, Mom and Dad saved the best for last." I stay below the radar and spend as much time as possible at Emily's house.

EMILY RECOMMENDS I come down to the restaurant where she works for an interview with her aunt, who trains waitresses at Elby's. The popular family restaurant is the cornerstone of our community. It sports a larger-than-life "Big Boy." The chubby, plastic mascot is featured in all of their ads, and I'm unsure if it's the youngster who's "big" or the plastic hamburger he hoists on a tray to greet hungry patrons at the entrance. Emily enjoys waitressing, saves money, and gets out of the house. Why not?

I'm hired right away—my first real job. The establishment is not far from our neighborhood, and I occasionally even walk to work. But I have no idea being on my feet for eight hours will make my headaches seem mild in comparison. By the end of the shift, my feet are like lead weights; my heels and the soles of my feet pulsate in my shoes. My toes scream, "Take me out of these leather torture chambers!" I eventually get used to the physical demands, but I no longer walk to work. I waitress all summer and into the fall. My top dresser drawer fills with dollar bills, some fives, and a few twenties. Tips are my new friend.

One day when the restaurant's crowded, one of the owners, Mr. Ellis Boury, comes in with his family and takes a booth. As I wait on nearby tables, I feel his stare. He has a reputation for scrutinizing the waitresses. My hands grow clammy, but I concentrate on my performance as I rush to serve my tables. I'm especially polite and professional to each group of customers. As he's leaving, Mr. Boury stops at my waitress station and watches me rinse out my cleaning cloth at the sink. I smile. He asks me my name.

A few minutes later, I'm called to the manager's office. My manager, Mary Lee, demands respect from her cooks and waitstaff. She's smiling as she tells me to take off my waitress apron; I'm being promoted to hostess. My job got me out of the house and let me earn some money, which has been great on both accounts. But, this promotion gives me a certain status and is a real shot to my self-esteem. As a waitress I make great tips, but the hostess has responsibility and respect that waitresses don't. I take ownership of the role, as if this is my very own diner.

During a particularly slow evening shift, I'm shocked to see my parents walk in. Mom and Dad seldom go out to eat, and this family restaurant doesn't serve alcohol. They carry in their own mixed drinks with kitchen-napkin coasters clinging to the bottoms. They're drunk. I'm mortified. They set their drinks on the table at their booth. I look around to see if anyone on the waitstaff notices. I hover over my parents and wave away the waitress that's assigned to their booth. I tell her that since it's slow I'll take this order. I pretend they're regular customers. I'm afraid that their drinks will be discovered, and they'll be asked to leave. They aren't. I'm embarrassed, but the news of my promotion to hostess was too much. They had to see their youngest in action.

BY MY LATE TEENS, I've withdrawn from parents. And, I seldom know where Hannah or John are. Mom and Dad don't keep tabs on John either, but if he's in his room at night, they rest easy. When he crashes at a friend's house, he calls home, and lets Mom know. I begin calling home; I say I'm staying at Emily's whether I am or not.

During the worst years, Dad's on John's case day and night. My brother and I grow distant. His drug use scares me. When we're both at home and I look at him, his guilty expression speaks to me: "I know you don't approve, Salou." He smiles, but his glassy, wasted eyes piss me off more.

"Don't smile at me!" I withdraw even further and try to shame him into looking honestly at himself. My words are as harsh as I can make them. "Why do you always have to act like this? You look gross!" I get in his face. I don't want Mom and Dad to hear. He stomps out of the room.

John's abuse of illegal substances is far more advanced than my own drinking. I'm terrified by his use of psychedelic drugs. I'd heard of people jumping off of tall buildings when they're high, believing they can fly. A Bethany College student jumps from the clock tower and dies.

I keep busy. I socialize. I do my schoolwork. I see John when he comes home to crash. We acknowledge each other, but I no longer seek him out. At the ice rink, I skate past him, note who he skates with, ask him how he's getting home, or who he came with. But our earlier, twin-like closeness is severed, as if a surgeon has cut us apart.

He gets caught running out of a restaurant with his friends without paying the bill. There's no telling what other kinds of trouble he gets into. After he graduates high school, John departs for the West coast—as far from West Virginia as he can get. Mom and Dad are no doubt relieved.

I don't blame him. No matter how much John has matured, home life has been a long series of abuses. Dad verbally assaults him every chance he gets—about his behavior, his appearance, and his grades. Even after John takes a woodworking class and shows proficiency with tools, Dad finds fault. There's no pleasing him. Also, Dad has an entitlement mentality. He drums it into us, especially John. On the rare occasion my brother tries to defend himself, Dad spits back: "How dare you defy me, after all my hard work!"

By the time he's eighteen, John stands toe-to-toe with Dad. At six foot two, they're eye to eye, and both of them take pride in who they've become as men. But Dad is the boss you can never please. It makes perfect sense for John to go west and to work with his hands. He has skills, thankfully. And, he'll fit right into the Western ethos with his rolled cigarettes, long hair, and easy-going nature.

He hitchhikes from Wheeling to Oregon; then, California. He finds work logging. He buys a used truck and drives back to Oregon, then to

Washington State. He makes friends easily, works hard, and takes pride in his work.

When he's out of sight, John is out of mind. I seldom think of him. I'm into my own activities. I play a leading role in *Barefoot in the Park* with a handsome leading man and a popular student. And, when my boyfriend, David, calls, we go out. I keep up with the light senior-year load, hang out at Emily's house, and go to spontaneous parties around bonfires out at the creek. I haven't a care in my world.

. . . I wake up Christmas morning in my own vomit, but I'm too hungover to move. My hair's matted and stuck to my pillowcase. I could have aspirated vomit and ended up asphyxiated. I smell terrible but am too sick to move. Mom stands at my bedroom door. She can smell me. "I hope you learned your lesson." It's a while before I get out of bed, shower, and strip the bed.

As my drinking progresses, alcohol poisoning becomes routine. I struggle out of bed, my head pounding as if Lebanon's town hall clock is clanging inside my skull. I walk around in a daze. Moving makes me dizzy and nauseated. I vomit.

I begin a new ritual. I'm smart—I figure I'll start taking two Excedrin tablets each evening before my first drink . . .

Switching Allegiances

DURING THE LONG WINTER OF 1977, my senior year, I meet my future husband at the Checkerboard, a neighborhood bar hangout. The snow's deep. School's been canceled for weeks. Grant and I make eyes at each other from across the room. When he stands up to walk over to where I'm seated, I notice how tall he is. At least six foot three. When he invites me to watch him challenge his friends to a pinball game, I can see why he has so many friends. It's not just the pinball machine that he takes command of. It's his audience, too. Their remarks, the laughter, the way they acquiesce to their tall, blond friend is unmistakable. *Is he this good at everything he touches,* I wonder? When he opens the door for me, he brings his face in a little close to mine and I melt. I feel very special. But I also sense a cautionary hesitance inside my mind: I'm six years younger than he. I should play hard to get. *Don't let on how hard you're falling. Let him lead. If he calls, when the phone rings, don't answer right away. Let Mom get it. When she calls out, "Sarah, it's for you," don't rush for the phone.*

Grant makes me laugh, and it becomes so easy just being around him and his friends. His eyes begin to linger, and I fall totally in love with him. I realize I already know his mom, Margie. At one time, I'd worked after school and on weekends at the shop where she had her hair done.

Margie loves me from the start. Maybe because she has four boys and always longed for a daughter. She doesn't know my family, but she is good friends with Hannah's sister-in-law, Freda, who owns the beauty shop. After Grant and I date awhile, Margie asks me if I have a brother John. She had picked him up in her Cadillac one winter when he was hitchhiking. She tells me how nice he was, how polite, and how handsome. I'm shocked they've met and that she's given him a ride across town. But it's common for young guys to hitchhike out on the highway, and Margie has a soft heart. I feel even more of a connection with her.

After a yearlong courtship, Grant and I elope. We don't project that a wedding might bring John home, though I want my brother to know Grant and to see me as an adult in my new life. I want him to visit my new home and see my new car. The thought of me visiting him out West never crosses my mind. Grant works six days a week, and we have no savings. Even if we could visit John, I fear what condition he'd be in. I'm content not knowing. Between the ages of eighteen and twenty-two, I live in a bubble. I am the center of my world. I know very little about Hannah and her husband, who's still in the air force. I've no idea where he's stationed. John's whereabouts in the Pacific Northwest are a mystery. On occasion, I miss him terribly.

"Sarah, did you know John's back in town?" Mom occasionally informs me. If I'm at Mom and Dad's, and John stops by, I feel I'm welcoming a stranger. I'm nervous about seeing him, maybe even afraid I'll run into him. It's likely he's in town only briefly anyway. I hate that awkward feeling around him. Maybe if he doesn't summon me, I might not even see him this time.

His brief visits disturb me. He looks like a bewildered hippie, his hair long and unkempt; he's pierced his ear with a needle and keeps rough thread dangling out of the hole. He hops trains to get back to West Virginia. He looks the part with his grimy face and Elvis grin, but he seems satisfied to have made it home. Despite his lanky thinness, hazy eyes, and poor posture, Mom and the rest of the family herald his homecoming as a special family event. Maybe it's time we have a family reunion.

Mom and Dad convince Granny, my Dad's sister and her family, and all of my siblings and their families to join us at Oglebay Park for a daylong family reunion.

When John returns to the West, I again lose touch with him. Weeks, sometimes months, pass when no one hears from him or knows where he is. He might call to tell us, "I'm in Ben Lomond, California," or "Big Sur is so incredible!" Next, he's in Washington, then Oregon, then back to Washington, where a logging company on Whidbey Island hires him for the season.

It's late summer when John visits again and stays with friends. He's almost twenty. He stops by the house when I'm there. Mom and Dad greet him with a hug and a handshake. John rolls his own cigarettes and sprinkles hashish in with the tobacco. He smokes his drug in front of Mom and Dad, and gets high. They haven't a clue. Dad and John speak civilly to one another. They seem to have mended their differences.

"How long are you here for?" Dad asks.

"Just a few days."

"Where are you staying?"

"My friend has a cabin up at Oglebay," John says. He looks at me. "You should come see me." I shrug. He'd already told me he uses hallucinogens: he makes tea from peyote buttons. Am I supposed to think peyote is cool? I have no desire to visit John in his new state of mind. Our parents accept his living arrangements. I go about my business.

The next day, I'm washing Mom's car in the driveway when I see John walking down Route 88. He's walking a bicycle and limping badly. When he walks onto the driveway, I can see that his eyes are glassy and dazed. His blue jeans are badly torn. I see blood from a long red and purple contusion that runs the length of his right thigh. It's so swollen, I don't know how he stands on it. His jeans are stuck to the blood. But he's smiling, pointing to the sky, mumbling. He tries not to stand on the bad leg. *Could it be broken?*

"Don't move!" I tell him and run indoors. I tell our parents I'm taking John to the emergency room. On the drive over, he talks nonsense. "You see the sky up there?" He points out the front windshield. "I painted that sky today, Sarah. I did! Isn't it beautiful?" I clench my teeth and grip the steering wheel.

"I don't want to hear it, John." I spit out the words. I try to bring him back to reality. He's a stranger to me. His drugged mind gives me the creeps.

I drop him off at the emergency room door and drive around to park. I don't care how much pain he might be in or how damaged his leg is. When I enter the hospital, the admissions director points me in the direction of his examining room. By the time I find him, he's already seen a doctor. I walk over to the gurney he's sitting on. He's still delusional.

"Did you hear that foreign doctor talking to me?" He's smiling through his drug-induced fog. "I understood his language. He was speaking in his native tongue, and I understood every word!" Though he's suffered a major contusion and torn some tendons, John feels no pain. He's bandaged and released. I take him to the place he's been staying and drop him off. It's another turning point in my wounded relationship with John. I'm upset over the incident and furious with him. I want nothing more to do with him. I feel he's crossed over to the dark side. If his drugs make him think he's some kind of god, heaven help him. "Painted the sky," he says. The drugs are talking for him, and they have him wound so tight I might never get him back. He leaves soon again for the West and is gone for another year.

WHEN HE NEXT RETURNS TO WHEELING, it's early fall. He calls me. "Hey, Salou, come visit me," he says. His voice sounds different—tender, even rational. I have known his moods so well; whether he's sad, confused, teary-eyed, or blissfully stoned, I can always tell. I've never seen him angry, except when Dad hit him, but John bottles it up, then tries to smoke and drink it all away.

Over the phone, I gauge his coherency. I conclude I can handle him today. My life has gone in new directions: married, my schedule revolves around Grant, who sells cars, and his friends. I'm getting ready to take college courses. But the afternoon John calls, I'm free.

As I drive up to the cabin, I'm glad John sounded so clear on the phone. No surprises this time. He even sounded eager to see me. I find the rustic cabin, one of Oglebay Park's original cabins with thin walls and no heat, at the end of a long, private gravel road. Most of these cabins have been replaced by more modern dwellings, but this one seems well suited for my hippie brother. There's a small fireplace. How fortunate John has a friend who will loan him the free space. Winter's only weeks away. Nights at the park come close to freezing, but John makes a living roughing it. I shrug off any worry about him getting cold. There's a small stack of firewood on the porch. It should suffice. John will head west again soon.

John greets me at the screen door. When I enter, he pulls me in close for a hug. I hug him back. He seems taller and thinner. He sits down and lights one of his homemade cigarettes. He offers me one. "No thanks." He gets quiet. He hangs his head and looks away. I sense this isn't a social visit. He looks deeply distressed, close to tears. "What's wrong, John?"

"You remember what was done to us when we were kids, back in Virginia?" He names the neighborhood pervert. My heart pounds. My throat tightens up. I'm at a loss for where this conversation is headed.

"That nasty creep? Are you serious?"

"Maybe for you it is nothing, but not for me." He looks down at the wood floor. "I can't get over it. It haunts me all the time." His voice trails off. He looks up at me and back down at the floor. "I question myself. Am I even a man." His shoulders are shaking. He wipes away tears. His pain is palpable. Is there more to the history with that neighbor than he's telling me? He turns to me again. "That guy, Salou, he paid me a quarter every time. I let him use me!" He cries. He looks so ashamed, as if he'd been the cause.

I have no words of consolation, no wisdom, no magic cure for his tortured soul. An uncomfortable silence permeates the room. All the life has been sucked out. I feel deep sadness and complete helplessness. I have no solution. He never told anyone about what he'd endured. He'd hinted to me that one time about his knowledge of sex, but I hadn't put two and two together. That the sexual abuse still torments him shocks me. He looks so fragile, like he might disintegrate.

"That's ancient history! It's all behind us now." What I say must sound to him like, "Forget it, man! Get over it!" My ill-chosen words seem to exacerbate his hopelessness.

We sit in silence a few minutes. He changes the subject. He asks what I've been up to. We talk about nothing. He stands up, signaling it's time for me to leave. We hug briefly. I walk away from the cabin and get into my car shaking my head, wondering how he will find closure.

His revelation throws me. What is history to me, is torturing John in the present day. The same lowlife who molested me, until I told on him, lured my innocent brother and abused him again and again, leaving my brother feeling complicit. John took his shame with him from Lebanon to Wheeling to Washington and back again.

Only God knew the extent of John's private hell, the confusion and shame that were compounded by our father's abuse. I've heard it said that shame is Satan's signature. Now I understand. Shame is like a tattoo on John's heart, making him vulnerable to attacks and self-deprecating. I don't tell anyone in the family what John said. It seems too personal and private—too painful a secret and not for me to divulge.

John returns to Washington. Is he a drug addict? Or is he in such turmoil, he uses drugs to forget? In *Permanent Midnight*, a painful memoir of a former heroin addict, I read: "You have to understand where drugs can take you. How the once unthinkable becomes routine and the routine, once established, is something you can never, ever think about. You never have to if you have the drugs."

AS BEFORE, we don't hear much from John. He lives in his truck, hops trains, changes jobs. When we speak, he tries to sound upbeat. But he only calls when he's having a good day. His continued drug use, plus the out-of-sight, out-of-mind reality, sever our bond.

John returns for Christmas when he's twenty-one. He carries gifts for everyone, 2600 miles across the country. He hitchhikes, grabs a seat on an open freight train. I imagine he's walked a long way, too. He's all smiles when we open his gifts. For me, he's brought a wooden, folding dish rack.

I hand him our infant, Amy Lynn, who was born with a birth defect. She sleeps soundly, all bundled up in his lanky arms. But when John goes west again, he and I are estranged, geographically and emotionally.

Amy's problems are very rare, the doctors say. Her condition, a seizure disorder, requires strong drugs that are too much for her little body. She can't breathe well when she's breastfeeding. She doesn't make eye contact. She doesn't smile. She fails to thrive. Her doctor tells me her organs are likely suffering. Still, I believe she will live for years, though she'll be handicapped and need assistance all her life. The specialists, therapies, and medicines seem to make matters worse. One morning, her little fingertips look blue. I call her doctor. He says to bring her in immediately. She has developed pneumonia.

Finally, Grant and I stand witness to her steady decline in intensive care. The doctor takes us to a private room and warns us, "I've brought Amy back twice already. She's had kidney failure and heart failure. I won't revive her again. If by some miracle she pulls through this, and I doubt she will, then we'll see."

He's matter-of-fact, as Grant and I sit there stunned. We prepare ourselves as best we can to lose her. For three days, she lies in an oxygen tent with Grant and me at her side. She's six months old and weighs only thirteen pounds. She doesn't respond to stimuli. Nothing helps. But we have time to say good-bye, and Amy dies peacefully. Grant and I grieve deeply and tenderly, and go on as best we can with support from our families.

I begin classes part time in Parkersburg. Still in West Virginia, we make a new life in St. Mary's. Every few months, I hear from John. We write superficial letters back and forth. Another year passes.

"WE'RE AVERAGING between 1200 and 1400 trees a day, which is pretty good, really," John writes in March 1981. "I built a house on the back of my truck with a couple of windows and a door, a bunk, a wood stove, and a refrigerator. Pretty cozy once I get a fire in it . . . . Once this job is up, I might fly home for a visit and even make it to Griffith's Lodge for my five-year class reunion—see what's shakin' when the time comes . . ." John's also proud of a fence he's installed for a woman named Lily O'Brien. In early May 1981, he writes, "Mrs. O'Brien and I are going salmon fishing next Sunday (Mother's Day) over on the peninsula." I'm so pleased to hear he works for someone with such a pleasant name, and I'm not surprised he's made a good impression on her. His newsy letter continues, "She's got a beach house in Useless Bay that she wants me to remodel for her this summer. Right below it is Mutiny Bay which got its name because when the boats came in, the sailors saw what a nice way of life the Indians were living there, and time after time the shipmates would commit mutiny, and refuse to return to sea and leave the paradise they found there." His new return address: General Delivery, Hood River, Oregon. But weeks go by with no more word from him.

Despite the upbeat tone of his last letter, I know John lives on the fringe. His experimenting with psychedelics—mushrooms he tells me—has never ceased. He still hallucinates. It's all affecting his judgment

During one of John's last visits home, I hear second-hand from Ed (or someone John talked to) that John overdosed on drugs out West, and was revived by having his stomach pumped. Supposedly, some man challenged him to a contest of wills that included drug tolerance. John insisted he was so spiritual that no amount of pills would affect him in the least. After John downed a handful of drugs, he was hospitalized. I never confront him about the story, but I know at that point, there is no drug he considers unsafe.

Devastation

THE MIDDAY SUN hides behind a cluster of clouds when the Mason County sheriff slowly pulls his cruiser into the driveway of my parents' home, which is now in rural New Haven, West Virginia. It's June, 1981.

"Who in hell's name?" Mom says, craning her neck to see outside.

"Looks like the goddamn sheriff," Dad replies, his hand on the heavy drapes. Two uniformed officers exit their nondescript gray vehicle and slowly make their way toward the door. Dad rises from his seat on the sunken couch in the smoke-filled room; he steadies himself to prepare for the intrusion. Some kind of official visit. "I paid my taxes." He clears his throat and snuffs out his cigarette.

Mom freezes at the insistent knock. She pleads with Dad, "You answer it."

Folks in these parts seldom use their front door. As Dad undoes the bolt, he looks out the two small windows on the top of the door. The officers have paused to remove their hats. Neighbors are at their windows. Bad news travels fast.

Dad pulls open the stiff entrance.

"Mr. Blizzard?" The one with the shiny badge stares straight at Dad, his tone serious.

"Yes, Sir," Dad's voice is steady. It's one thirty in the afternoon. Dad poured his first whiskey at eleven. Mom matches him drink for drink, but the sight of these men has sobered them up. Mom puts out her cigarette and stands behind her husband of forty years.

"Come in." Dad opens the door wide, ushering the officers inside.

"I'm sorry to have to tell you this, sir, but we have bad news concerning your son John Edward."

"What has he done, Officer?"

"No, sir, your son's not in any trouble. His body—his remains—have been recovered from a river in Washington State."

I receive the phone call later that evening at my home in St. Mary's, West Virginia, after Dad has already called Rosemary, Molly, Ed, and Hannah.

"Sarah, John's gone." Dad's voice shakes on the other end. I hold the phone tight to my ear, not sure I understand.

"What do you mean 'he's gone' . . . where did he go?"

"He's dead." Dad's words trail off down a long tunnel. My breath pulses in my ear. I clutch the phone with one hand and grip the kitchen counter with the other.

"Who—who told you this?" I manage.

"Sheriff was just here. They discovered his body in a flooded river. Said he had all of his personal effects on him. They don't expect foul play." The words are empty of any semblance of reality.

I can hear Dad's beloved clocks ticking in the background, the entire collection striking the time. *Where's Mom*, I wonder? Is she listening to everything Dad says? Or is she in one of the ladder-back chairs next to the phone, her head on the kitchen table? Has she collapsed? Is she out of her mind in agony?

"He'd been missing from work for two weeks. Had his wallet on him. Everything intact. Nothing to investigate. They're shipping him to Dunbar."

I feel a gnawing bitterness and a smoldering resentment towards Dad, and something worse aimed at myself. Dad's to blame for this.

John was his scapegoat. It's his fault John's body was left to the elements. Emotions I've never known form a posse around me. They band against me, insulting, accusing. John sought me out for his midnight confession. I knew his worst secrets. I could have prevented his death. I neglected him as much as Dad did.

That is just the beginning. Was John out of his mind? Was he hazed out on drugs before he stumbled, fell, or jumped into those raging waters? No autopsy, with its toxicology tests, was ever performed, as best I know. He'd been missing from work, his body drifting away like discarded rubbish, but his two-week absence had set off no alarms?

I hang up the phone. I look out the back window. The quiet neighborhood and comfortable home I live in suddenly feels foreign. John's presence overwhelms me and calls out to me from the depths. I lean over the kitchen sink. The wooden drying rack John carried across the country and gave to me for Christmas years back sits on the counter holding clean dishes. The image of him holding Amy Lynn arises, now etched forever in my memory.

I shriek, "Grant!" My husband comes running and catches me in his arms. I babble incoherently about bringing John's body home. "I'm so sorry," he says, his strong arms around me.

WHILE WE WAIT for John's body to be shipped home, I simmer in an emotional cauldron of self-pity, self-blame, and resentment. I hold Dad responsible for not parenting John well enough to help him overcome his bad habits and for not responding to his need for a father's love and acceptance.

As I stand in the somber funeral parlor, I feel weak and empty. I can't eat; fitful sleep has left me sore all over. I shift my weight from one leg to the other, grabbing the back of an upholstered chair for support. My family members are clustered together. I avoid them and the awkward conversations. My stomach is in knots; my skin feels like it could crawl.

Beside John's closed casket, I stand as sentry, still guarding his secrets, resentful of everything and everyone who may have contributed to this moment, including myself. But no matter how angry I feel towards Dad, I recall my baby's death the previous year and I feel compassion towards both him and Mom. Our devastating loss of a child, which we saw coming, is of another order. John's death feels like a cruel hoax. I become distraught with an image of him struggling in the water, and I want to comfort him. Mixed in is a hopeless dread. How can I possibly face a future without him here?

This unquenchable ache to reconnect with John haunts me as I spy a small group of young men enter the back of the funeral home. Their presence makes this all too real. They trudge slowly forward, single file. Their heads down, they wear devastation on their sagging shoulders like a heavy cloak. I have no comfort to offer. There is nothing here, folks—no long curls on top of his blond head; no curly eyelashes or his long, straight nose; not his full lips, nor his well-worn flannel shirt, nor his faded, threadbare jeans; not his long hands and fingers that rolled his own cigarettes.

We all grew up together in Wheeling. They'd been John's advocates, his protectors; these are the guys with whom he'd hitchhiked down to Rosemary's home in Abingdon when they were all sixteen. The boys who knew him and loved him for who he was, and who knew most of his secrets, are all men now. They're dressed in button-down, collared shirts and ties, with dress slacks—instead of T-shirts and jeans. But John should be here, with his smile and the happy-go-lucky attitude he embraced whenever these guys were around.

The closer they get, the more uncomfortable I become. I avoid eye contact and grab myself with both arms across my chest. Then I reach out, eyes closed, and hug whoever's in the lead—Mike or Dan, Marc or Steve. For a brief moment, they bring John back to life. I hold on to somebody's shirt sleeve. Suddenly I need them all to be close. But as soon as they are, I fear I'll be swallowed up.

"Sarah, we're so sorry."

Weeping and trembling, I try to say something supportive, to put a voice to what it means to see them here. But the words get caught in my throat. I sob from my depths. If I'm supposed to be strong for them, I end up needing their consolation in that hollow place.

They say there are stages to grief, and the first is denial. I embrace it. Gripped by a lack of finality and clueless as to how desperately I'll need to sort this all out, my psyche acts like a drunken driver, randomly changing lanes, out of control.

I LOOK AT THE FUNERAL DIRECTORS in their suits and ties, standing in their clusters and avoiding eye contact. Family members mill about in slow motion. Mom sits weakly on a wood chair flanked by Rosemary and Molly. I stand apart in private anguish. Is John's body actually inside that casket? I don't feel his presence. Shouldn't I? His casket might be empty. I look to my family, but they're not seeing me. Have they all accepted that this is the way it is? Is there anyone who hasn't taken a swig from Rosemary's hidden, silver flask?

I can't accept that not seeing John's dead body spares us gruesome horrors. I'm angry towards the funeral director who withholds John's presence from us. The closed casket signifies the cruelty of John's death, his aloneness. My faith keeps reassuring me that even though a person's cold, stiff body is on display, the deceased is not present, and the most valuable aspect of the person, their soul, has departed.

Even so, I go back and forth from anguished thoughts of John dying alone to weird fantasies that this is all a sickening hoax. Physically, emotionally, privately, I am convinced John's body might not actually be in that box. Denial balloons in my heart, and a deep-seated resentment fills the air inside.

In the ladies room, I run into Rosemary. We greet one another with a hug, then she reaches inside her purse and lifts out the flask. The moment she turns it up to take a swig, it catches the glare of the light over the mirror. That instant, I begin to pity her. I don't see her need for a drink as a dependence on alcohol; I see her running away from the fact that we must deal with our brother's death. I want somebody there, maybe a sibling, to acknowledge the level of pain we all feel.

I need a speech, a sermon, a heart-felt testimony—some validation of this reality. How else are we to face the fact that John had been missing for two whole weeks and none of us knew? Maybe some authority figure could help us confront the fact that he floated dead in that raging river for days on end.

To this day, none of us really know what happened. Did John take his own life? Unthinkable, if you knew the happy-go-lucky John we want to remember. But there was a dark side to my brother, made darker by the stronghold of shame he carried around with him for all those years— shame that only I know about.

John's former boss and a young woman John dated out West give post-death reports to our parents. They each say it wasn't unusual for John to not show up for work for days, even weeks. When he did appear, he was upbeat and energetic one day, and very down the next. I was not too surprised to hear details such as, "Trusting and fearless, John took chances. He saw the good in people, who then took advantage of him. John was plagued by unnamed demons . . ." Most disturbing to me is that, though he'd been missing for two weeks, they hadn't begun to check on him.

I'm in private turmoil, and the unresolved issue of John's sexual victimization churns in my soul. I feel terribly sorry for myself. My closest sibling, the one I'd longed to know as an adult but had given up on, the one with whom I'd shared my secrets, was dead. I can't reconcile this loss. I can't move forward. It's as if the director of our family play said, "Cut!" in the middle of a scene. We have no natural conclusion. I know my brother's secrets. They lead somehow to this tragic ending. I'm numb. I grieve in my heart and mind knowing John died without getting help for his anguish. We Blizzards have suffered heart-wrenching ordeals, but John's funeral is the most heart-wrenching of all. I can't accept losing him. John's death is a powerful kick in the gut.

I've always had vivid dreams, and after John's death, I enter an extraordinarily vivid dream phase. I call Hannah to report unbelievably believable scenes of a living John sitting in someone else's kitchen chair, at a party, smoking a rolled cigarette. I approach him, dumbfounded. He puts out his hand to fend me off. He shakes his head at me, and I back off, but I long to touch him. He says, "No, don't get too close." Then, "Don't tell Mom; I've had to be away." I step back in total shock. I'm certain the coroner has been mistaken. We've buried the wrong man!

The next dream, a week or so later, is similar. I see John at a friend's house, where he's been hiding out. "I didn't want to worry anyone," he says. Same story, dream after dream. Hannah cries. She says she doesn't know what to say. Thoughts of burying our brother torture her too.

I'm plagued by the dreams and by John haunting my daylight hours. I can't shake the feeling of having truly seen him, and the frustration of the fantasy. Could he actually be alive and the coroner horribly mistaken? Also troubling, the dreams are cautionary too: John doesn't want me to tell anyone.

A year later, Grant and I have a healthy baby girl who thrives. We move back to Wheeling when Grant's asked to take over his dad's business so he can retire. I volunteer at Crisis Hotline, a 24/7 call-in service. A professional psychologist, who deals with depressed patients as well as suicide prevention, talks to us about the possibility that we'll receive calls from people who are suicidal. He emphasizes how important it is to be good listeners, to reflect the caller's feelings back to him or her. If someone is determined to kill themselves, there's little any of us can do to change that. If we receive such a call, we're to listen, reflect, and delicately extract the location of the caller. No matter how the call goes, we're to call the psychologist at his home, day or night, if we need to talk afterward. We're not ever to check obituaries for the names of callers who have told us who they are.

"Over 95 percent of all juveniles we deal with have, at some point in their young lives, been sexually abused," he tells us. I catch my breath and think of John. Sexual abuse victims can be tended to, mended, and even healed under the right guidance. There's power in telling our stories. The enemy of our souls is a great deceiver. He would like for us all to live in shame, disgrace, and regret. John was unable to share his pain with a helpful counselor or receive any support. Nothing empowered him. John's secrets likely led him to the end of his life in Republic, Washington.

Our parents grieve privately. I hope Dad's going through hell. He's to blame that John never got help and was robbed of the life he deserved, and he's to blame that I feel cheated. John would never know my children, and they would never know their Uncle John. I seethe and replay my brother's torment in my mind.

Parallel Tracks

GRANT'S BEEN AWAY in the rehab program for two weeks. What will he do now?

Late one evening a few days after I've issued my ultimatum, Grant calls again. "I heard my story tonight."

"What do you mean?"

"A guy here . . . when he told his story . . . it could have been my own. Only he was a professional athlete, and lost everything because of his alcoholism: his career, his family, his money. His wife left him, but when he got straightened out she came back and now they both work a program." My heart pounds inside my chest as I hear my husband's emotions rising over the phone. "I've decided to stay. It's not going to be easy, but I want to try now."

St. Augustine said, "Hope has two beautiful sisters. Their names are anger and courage; anger at the way things are and courage to see that they do not remain the way they are." I have three actual sisters, and now I have two more: these two beautiful ones, which I begin to embrace.

JILL INVITES ME TO ATTEND the Family Program with her. We drive to Wernersville, Pennsylvania, where we join ten other spouses for five and a half days of intense counseling. While there, the staff recommends Grant and I meet face to face with two counselors in attendance. They know Grant; he's currently a resident. One asks me about our marriage, "When Grant returns home, what are your expectations?" It's a big, hard question, and it's one that I need help answering.

Soon after, in counseling together with Grant, I say, "I've always heard marriage should be 50–50."

My counselor smiles. She looks at Grant, then back at me. "It sounds to me like you two have a really good shot at success here. But what about each of you giving one hundred percent?" My heart opens to the possibilities. "Think of it like you're on a set of parallel railroad tracks, side by side. At times, he's going to be way out ahead of you. Other times, you'll be in the lead. But you'll always be side by side."

My counselor also nails me on my own drinking history. The safe environment enables me to be brutally honest about everything. It's recommended that I stay for twenty-eight days of treatment.

"I want to embrace this recovery thing, but our daughter has been without her dad for almost a month now. I'll take your recommendation home with me, and—like Grant— I'll attend AA meetings too." That's what I do. The Family Program certificate of graduation is a small banner I'm urged to display on our refrigerator. It reads, "You Are Important."

Grant completes more than thirty days of rehab and flies home on Valentine's Day, 1986. We become best friends again. After more than a month apart, we find we enjoy being sober lovers. We become more attentive parents.

"Let's go downtown and look at matching wedding bands." *Had someone from rehab confronted him about his lack of a wedding ring?* Though I'd been wearing a small band for eight years now, since Day One of our marriage, his lack of interest in wearing one was never my concern. His dad never wore one either, though his parents had a long marriage. So, when he suggests we go together for rings, it seems it's more for his peace of mind than my own. I gladly accept the invitation.

It's his first valiant effort in doing something completely different, and his gesture would come to symbolize our starting over. Seeing the new, shiny gold ring on his left hand gives me a strong sense of Grant's true commitment.

COMMUNICATION, THOUGH, IS CHALLENGING for us. I'm so used to Grant taking charge in life and in arguments that I'm clueless how to approach him with my own opinions. Over the course of that first sober winter, one of us, or both, pivots. The dynamics change, and I begin to feel I'm getting respect from Grant like I never have before. He listens. He doesn't always agree, but he's attentive. I respond with more loving displays of affection towards him. We regain a sense of humor; we laugh together. Grant has always had a quick wit and it's still there. Self-pity slips in a time or two, but he doesn't nurture it. He'd like to hang out with the guys down at Babe's Place, and I never stop him. But he's uncomfortable enough around alcohol that he voluntarily changes his plans. We both work at keeping our priorities fresh. We let go of some friendships that were based solely on drinking. I continue to attend AA meetings in Wheeling and out of town when I travel: noon meetings, evenings, women-only, and speaker meetings, which Grant and I enjoy together.

Grant's brother Richie and Richie's wife, Liz, are both in recovery and have been working a program for some time. Married into Grant's family, Liz is easy to get to know. With a history of health problems, she feels like she is living on borrowed time. She is friendly and easygoing, and later asks for me when she is dying. But during those early days of recovery for Grant and me, she and Richie are understanding, knowledgeable of AA and Al-Anon, and supportive of however we choose to pursue sobriety. Liz and I become friends, but when she shares anything about Al-Anon, she seems less an advocate than simply a person happy to have found it. When her husband attends meetings, she attends hers. It's their lifestyle. She's never pushy or expectant of us to follow their methods, though that's what I do.

IN JANUARY 2019, by the grace of God, Grant and I will have celebrated thirty-three years of sobriety. We've become adept at communicating without pointing fingers. We've kept our recovery journeys separate, watched our expectations of the other person, and learned to turn to our Twelve Steps sponsors. The most satisfying journey has been the one along parallel tracks.

Through working the Twelve Steps of Alcoholics Anonymous and Al-Anon, I began to face the losses and the emotions I had buried. But what was I to do with the pain once I dredged it up or with the gnawing regrets I felt over John's childhood—his sexual and emotional abuse? My anguish over his death wasn't going away. When I sought a counselor's advice, she suggested I write John a letter, as if he would find it in his post office box and read it.

When I got home that evening, I got out a pen and a blank sheet of paper. But as I thought about how and where to begin, I wept. I tortured myself with guilt over my childish tattling. I was stuck in our childhood. How would I ever work through my adulthood if I never got out of adolescence? Guilt ate away at me; my heart felt all broken over John. After weeks of emotional restlessness, I still couldn't pen the first word of my letter to John. That night, I fell into an exhausted, deep sleep. I dreamed something totally different, from some other realm:

I'm standing on a cloud out in space where there is no heaviness. John walks straight towards me, across the sky, as though he's walking through a wall. His face is open, his countenance devoid of any pain. He exudes peace. He immediately embraces me. Without any words, I begin communicating all the things I've had no time to say before. I convey how sorry I am about his life ending the way it has. I'm sorry for telling on him every chance I got and for how unfair I'd been. I say all of this to his face, but my mouth doesn't move and I don't make a sound. Our thoughts transfer from my heart to his heart, and back again. John looks perfect, complete; his embrace is so real, and it lasts just as long as I need.

"This is how I look now," he says. His face is more open than I ever remember; his eyes are clearer than his very best days on earth when we were free to laugh and be ourselves. After each apology I make, his embrace speaks of complete forgiveness for every earthly wrong that I've committed against him. He gently convinces me he is in no pain; he is quite well.

When I awoke, I knew I was changed. Heaven was so close I could practically touch it. I called Hannah to tell her, as best I could, the details of my incredible dream. She cried and thanked me for calling. The experience left me with a light heart. I didn't dread my dreams anymore. I realized I may never know the whole story of John's ending. But by the grace of God, I will one day see that sweet, young man again. Until then, I believe in my heart that he struggled to survive.

THE AUTHOR ZORA NEALE HURSTON'S words resonate with me: "If you are silent about your pain, they'll kill you and say you enjoyed it." Deep wounds can and do heal; I'm living proof. I set the worst memories aside in the scrapbook of my heart where I could deal with them.

Growing up in my Blizzard family was like being in a snowstorm at times. Visibility was low when it came to knowing what to do about the strongholds of alcoholism, abuse, and destructive tendencies.

Reconciling oneself to the causes and effects of abuse, of alcoholism, and of loss is personal, based on each individual's ability or willingness to face the pain. I couldn't resolve anyone else's issues, and honesty has been the key to my recovery. In Alcoholics Anonymous, there is this saying in the preamble: "There are those who cannot or will not completely give themselves to [the workings of] this simple program, usually men and women who are constitutionally incapable of being honest with themselves."

Recovery is regaining what you once had. How long had it been since I felt like myself, knew who I was, or had an optimistic view of where I was headed? Not since I first began experimenting with alcohol at age fourteen. At twenty-six, I began trying to recapture some sense of my self-worth.

At first, in addition to attending AA discussion group meetings, I sat on metal folding chairs in church fellowship halls at speaker meetings, listening to one brave speaker after another. Week after week, I heard stories that astounded me—not just for the person's dramatic descent into a completely unmanageable life but for the dramatic difference their recovery had made. They weren't guilt-ridden. I heard freedom in their voices. I tried not to compare my story to theirs, but many had the same relationship I'd had with alcohol: one was too many, and twenty was never enough. It wasn't until I actually heard a speaker say this, that I remembered my routine: I drank until the TV set above the bar got blurry. That was my end point.

I could even recall the testimony of a priest who came to speak to my high school when I was a freshman. We were all called into Central's cafeteria for his talk. The short, slightly built man in his priest collar stood before us and introduced himself as a recovered alcoholic. It may have been his thick Irish accent, but when he said that, there were snickers all around. He continued and recounted some of his drinking history. As a typical fourteen-year-old, I wasn't really paying very close attention to him, until he said, "The simplest definition of an alcoholic is a person who has problems as a result of their drinking." There were problems in my family. And though I'd never want my fellow students to see it and catch me, my ears perked up.

He went on to say there were times that—when he was still drinking—whenever he celebrated the mass with another priest, he became preoccupied with the wine left in the chalice after communion had been served. If his fellow priest got to the leftover wine before he did and drank the remainder—finishing off the blessed wine, as is required—the priest confessed, "It made me feel jealous. I formed a resentment." Looking back, he said, this was his alcoholic thinking.

LATER, OTHER TESTIMONIES STUCK WITH ME, even when I couldn't relate. One man recalled seeing/feeling bugs crawling up his arms, but none were actually there. Others had been in jail, in prison, divorced, destitute, and living—literally—under a bridge. I began to hear a still, small voice in my head: "There but by the grace of God go you." I heard, too, of these same people's authentic recoveries, with restored minds and restored relationships. Drunks who were threatened with losing their jobs got sober, and their careers were no longer on the line. Jail and imprisonment were no longer being held over their head. Physical health returned. No more tortured images of bugs crawling up their arms.

Many had been drinking for far longer than I had. I hadn't suffered dire consequences yet. But comparison was a trap, a tool of the enemy of my soul to draw me toward a conclusion that I am different and don't need these meetings. We alcoholics die if we continue to "suffer from terminal uniqueness."

Reading the preamble at every meeting included, "Anonymity is the spiritual foundation of all our principles, ever reminding us to place principles before personalities." I made up my own mind. I am here for me, not for Grant, not for John. Me. And maybe for our young daughter, who deserves an attentive mom. At each meeting, I heard the Serenity Prayer (God, grant me . . .). I'd always prayed and could still recite the Catholic prayers of my youth. But this prayer took an entirely different mindset: Could I begin to accept the people, places, and things around me that were beyond my control? Could I muster up the courage to be the person God intended me to be, with a mind of my own? And, could I rely completely on God for wise guidance where every aspect of my life was concerned—the past, present, and future?

"God, grant me the serenity to accept the things I cannot change; courage to change the things I can; and wisdom to know the difference."

I began to apply these principles even before I answered the phone or the front door, not knowing who might be on the other end wanting something from me, maybe even an explanation. The prayer helped me draw my first, healthy boundaries with Grant, and with others. And I began to understand the word *serenity* on a very deep level.

At one AA meeting, the topic was "dry people, dry places." I got the nerve to share that I intended to stay away from the bar scene, the drinking parties—"to avoid the near occasion of sin," as we used to say in the Catholic church. But then I asked, "How am I to handle it, if I find myself in a drinking situation?" The answer came. My sobriety must come first. If I'm invited to a gathering where alcohol is being served, make sure three criteria are met: Number one: Is there a good reason for me to be there? Family/school reunion, a wedding, a celebration of some kind? Number two: What's my spiritual condition like—do I feel close to my Higher Power? Number three: Is there someone with me who knows my condition?

After months of meetings, where I heard brutal honesty, it clicked. But could I be as honest? Just because I had never experienced many of alcoholism's grave consequences such as an arrest, a divorce, or losing a job, hadn't I come close? Hadn't I lost enough? If I were asked to speak at a meeting, to give my own story, could I share what the disease had taken from me?

I IMAGINE A CAUTION in "Parenting 101:" Don't make any flagrant mistakes, or your children will grow up to write books about you. Writers raised in alcoholic homes can develop and record some pretty damaging material. While writing, we may be faced with the ways in which we've begun to repeat the patterns set up for us before we were even born. In some cases, we are third- and fourth-generation unhealthy. If my parents were alive to read these accounts, would they be outraged? Could they be honest with themselves? More importantly, am I being honest? I know, denial of my own weaknesses while blaming others is part of this insidious disorder.

This is where working Step One, with its candor, became very clear: "Admitting we were powerless over alcohol, that our lives had become unmanageable." I was ready to face the truth and share with a group when I was asked to give my first lead as a speaker. It seemed a huge risk. I envisioned the worst that could happen: people getting up and walking out of the room once I told my story. But it never happened. In the safety net of a Twelve Steps group setting, I let down my guard and trusted the process. I made my shortcomings available, praying "Lord, help me to say what You want them to hear." Telling my story was freeing for me, and I hoped it could help free someone else.

I was starting to see how the "twelve promises," which are read at the end of AA meetings, were being fulfilled in my life: ". . . Fear of people and economic insecurities will leave us. . . . We will intuitively know how to handle situations that used to baffle us. . . . We will suddenly realize that God is doing for us what we could not do for ourselves."

Fear of what others might think could have crippled me. But in the safety of the recovery-group dynamic, I allowed the process to work in me, to re-awaken the pain. Fear took its rightful back seat and even motivated me. I'd faced real fear before: Giving birth felt like dying. Labor pain was so terrifying that, during labor, I, like many women, held my breath. I was determined to give birth naturally, with no drugs. I gripped the sheet like a vise, wanting to cautiously tread into this new phase of hard labor, but my body was thrusting me, like a carnival ride gone bad. I was sure the next contraction would touch ground! The nurse—or midwife or coach—reminded me to breathe. But I knew the next contraction could kill me. The anticipation hit me square between the eyes. No matter how many billions of women had already lived through this, I felt like the first person to have ever suffered in this way.

POWERLESSNESS HAD VISITED ME more times than I knew how to cope: the unforeseen problems and death of my first baby plus the sudden death of my closest brother—all had left me on such shaky ground, I thought it might one day swallow me up. Looking directly at my part in each loss, feeling the feelings, helped me move forward. I went back to church and found a welcoming congregation. Sermons took on new meaning, as if they were written for me. Grant and I joined a Sunday School class and enjoyed the fellowship. We both learned to let go.

I seldom divulged my participation in AA and AL-Anon, unless by the providential hand of God, I felt especially compelled to share. I became a student of God's word. My faith grew, and I found the adage I'd heard in the meetings to be true: "Religion cannot enhance the Twelve Steps. But the Twelve Steps can enhance any religion." I was sober by the time Mom died from cancer in her late sixties. Sober, I watched Rosemary, with a highball in the morning, when everyone else was drinking coffee. I even wrote her a long letter, in which I shared my new-found sobriety. She never acknowledged my letter. It was too late.

Epilogue

EARLY ONE SUMMER, after we've lived in Mississippi a couple of years, Dad calls me from Virginia where he lives with his new wife, Janet. Mom has passed away from cancer, when they've been married forty-nine years. "I'd like to come visit you folks, if it's not too much trouble. Janet's not feeling quite up to making the trip, so it'll just be me."

I pick him up at the airport, and Dad spends a weekend hanging out with us—Grant and me, and our youngsters. We now have three little girls. Dad repairs and oils every squeaky door hinge and clock in the house. We take walks to the harbor to feed the ducks. We walk past Senator Trent Lott's house so Dad can tell Janet it's true: the man she listens to on CNN is our neighbor. Dad tells both Grant and me how proud he is of us, and how much he enjoys being with our family. He mentions in passing what a shame it was to lose John the way we did. What words, coming from Dad! So different from the ones he'd used during our formative years. But time spent working the Twelve Steps has healed my broken heart. I no longer dwell on anger and resentment towards Dad. I feel a new kind of freedom with myself—and with Dad.

He seems pretty comfortable with our family's routine—including not drinking—and with following our schedule, except when it's time to go to church. Sunday morning, the day he is going to fly home, we're dressing for the church service. Dad's flight doesn't depart until late that afternoon, so I invite him to join us.

"No thanks. Didn't pack a tie." I grab one of Grant's ties and offer it to him. Dad accepts. He ties it across the neck of his shirt and comes along. When the congregation stands to recite the Nicene Creed, Dad remains seated.

Later, on the drive to the airport, he asks, "Sarah, you know that part of the service where you all stood up, said all those things?" I smile. "You mean, 'I believe in God, the Father Almighty, Maker of heaven and earth . . .'?"

"Yeah. I don't believe a word of it. Not one word."

He catches me off guard, but I don't hesitate. "Well, Dad, that's your prerogative. You can believe whatever you want."

"You believe all that?" he asks.

"Oh, yes sir, I do; every word. And you know what else? I think you and I have more in common than you think, where faith is concerned. Take heaven, for instance. I've seen you, surrounded by your grandchildren. You get such joy deep down in your heart from just watching them, from loving them. I've seen tears in your eyes. From the sheer magnitude of it all, from how deeply you feel love for your family. That love never dies. Dad, that's a taste of heaven right there."

He just nods. "Well, yeah." And we go off in some other direction.

The entire weekend, I have this overwhelming feeling that Dad has come to make amends. And he does, in his own way. There is closure in my heart; I forgive him—for the abuse, for the neglect, for what happened to John. I desire only peace for him.

NEAR THE END OF ROSEMARY'S LIFE, Ed becomes very concerned about her living alone in an apartment in Abingdon. He drives to her house from his place in Cincinnati and finds her suffering from a relentless nosebleed. He drives her back to his home, hoping to get her help. He calls an ambulance. She's admitted to the hospital and given a death sentence: bleeding out from advanced cirrhosis. Her hospice stay is a grueling and painful wait for her death.

Ed champions his own fight against cancer, surviving years of debilitating treatments. He goes to chemotherapy wearing his jeans with a dress shirt, tie, and leather vest. He misses very little work and even travels long distances to be with family members just weeks before he passes away.

In 2003, Dad dies in his mid-eighties of cancer. Ed, in 2014. Only Molly, Hannah, and I remain. We meet periodically to reconnect. We sit at Molly's kitchen table for hours, with Robby nearby, going through family photographs. We talk about the pain of our losses, like splinters that only hurt when you touch them. We share our individual grief: Molly had more history with Rosemary and Ed; Hannah and I had more history with John. When your once-large family dwindles in number, questions arise that are difficult to resolve. I see a strong connection between our maternal grandfather's untimely death at twenty-three and John's at the same age. Though their deaths were fifty-seven years apart, alcohol or drugs were likely involved in both.

There is a big difference in the level of openness with which each generation chooses to deal with its tragedies. If Mom had been as forthright as I about the poor choice her father had made seeking his beloved moonshine when he had a wife and three young children at home, would our family have had a different perspective on the dangers of drinking? In both generations, our family has been left with unresolved issues as they relate to the disease of alcoholism and drug addiction. Honest, soul-searching dialogue, within the walls of recovery and as a participant in one of my church's small groups, helps me sort out the effects of generational strongholds. The lack of honesty in confronting my shortcomings—the poor choices, the selfish decisions before recovery, and my pride—contributes to the years I nurtured my disease, whose middle name is denial.

One of the many rewards for staying sober and working the Twelve Steps is knowing how to handle situations that used to baffle me. *Baffle* is a great word. Our family's untimely deaths left us all confused, bewildered, and mystified at times.

If we were to offer a eulogy of our past, we Blizzards might agree, over time, how we've healed from each loss—some losses more than others. But the pain never completely subsides. At times, it reawakens like a fresh wound, replacing any numbness with gut-wrenching tears and sadness that won't lift. Valued lives and cherished friends have slipped away.

In years and years of writing poetry and fiction, I've been drawn to my childhood recollections. In looking at my life story, I agree with Mary Karr in *The Art of Memoir*: "With characters as good as these, why make shit up?" Indeed, I had "good characters." And, similar to Yeats's experience—"Mad Ireland hurt me into poetry"—I turned my hurt into memoir, as my heart typed out my brain's recordings. But, would I have the nerve to tell it? I got my final nudge—permission, if you will—from Jerry Stahl who wrote in *Permanent Midnight*, "If you had to live it, you get to write it." But, not just write it but share it.

IF IT'S TRUE that we are as sick as our secrets, we can have compassion for those who are unable to face them. My brother John was either unwilling or unable to face the hidden demons, but I have met countless of wounded men and women who are recovering from such.

I've learned about their lives as I sat inside random meeting rooms. One met on Wednesdays, at noon. By twelve-o'clock sharp, the long tables—set up in a rectangular fashion so that we could all make eye contact—were full of strangers: former misfits, dreamers, homeless, wanderers, teenagers wearing court-ordered ankle bracelets, young mothers with their babies in carriers, the elderly, and intellectuals in three-piece suits. I've gained unmerited strength from listening to them tell their stories in the safe environment of the Twelve Step program. I've heard a pin drop as the chairperson, an absolute legend from New York (word was, she got sober with Bill W., the founder of AA) shared her experience, strength, and hope.

I fought the urge to make comparisons, lest I go the way of "terminal uniqueness." And in telling my own story, I've learned to "give myself to this simple program" and to be honest with myself and others. I've learned what it means to truly forgive myself, and I've made progress in forgiving others.

At a critical juncture in my journey, I realized quite clearly that I could live and learn—or, I could learn and live.

The battle was over. A new perspective grabbed hold of me, and I went forward as if with blinders on, embracing the physical, emotional, and spiritual rewards of sobriety. I began to face the world on its own terms with new confidence. The journey continues.

IN OUR BLIZZARD FAMILY, a new age has begun—an age delivering grandbabies in spades. When they toddle up to our knees, we lift them into our laps, tousle their hair, and kiss their chubby cheeks while their hearts beat the rhythm of our ancestry. In spite of our shared grief, with each loss, we've navigated a new beginning. Some of us may even rewrite our own ending, and accept each other's chosen paths along the way.

Acknowledgments

THIS BOOK would not have come to be without the support and encouragement of my husband. Through your keen eye and careful reading, you have suggested edits that have been invaluable in bringing this book to fruition. Our three daughters have given honest feedback and been a source of great inspiration.

To the members of WV Writers, especially my mentor Mary Lucille DeBerry for saying I would one day write a memoir, your talent and insight have made this book possible.

I am grateful to those who have published my work elsewhere, especially those pieces informed by my life story, and which appear in *Voices from the Attic*, "Diner Stories: On the Menu," and *Heartwood Literary Magazine*.

To the brilliant, tireless Ginny Cunningham, Rae Jean Sielen, and Andrew Rorabaugh, for your editorial assistance. Your expertise has helped me see my work with new eyes and bring this story to life for the reader. It's been an honor to have worked with Populore.

SARAH BLIZZARD is an active writer who enjoys composing creative nonfiction in the form of poetry and memoir, and who participates in local writing groups and workshops, including with WV Writers and Osher Lifelong Learning Institute at West Virginia University. Her work has been featured in a number of print and online publications.

Sober and free since 1986, Sarah uses her writing as a therapeutic tool to express her gratitude for her recovery from alcoholism. She also mentors other women in recovery.

She considers participation in Bible study a vital personal discipline, and claims Psalm 40:1–2 as a taste of God's redemptive work in her life.

I waited patiently for the Lord;
he turned to me and heard my cry.
He lifted me out of the slimy pit,
out of the mud and mire.
He set my feet on a rock
and gave me a firm place to stand.

Sarah has been married to the love of her life for over forty years, and enjoys every moment spent with her three grown daughters, her sons-in-law, and three granddaughters.

Made in the USA
Columbia, SC
08 October 2018